THE
FULFILLMENT
OF
PASSOVER
AND
THE
TIMELINE OF THE CRUCIFIXION
OF
JESUS
CHRIST

COMMON MAN'S
COMMENTARY

GENE MADIA

WESTBOW
PRESS®
A DIVISION OF THOMAS NELSON
& ZONDERVAN

This book is a work of non-fiction. Unless otherwise noted, the author and the publisher make no explicit guarantees as to the accuracy of the information contained in this book and in some cases, names of people and places have been altered to protect their privacy.

WestBow Press books may be ordered through booksellers or by contacting:

WestBow Press
A Division of Thomas Nelson & Zondervan
1663 Liberty Drive
Bloomington, IN 47403
www.westbowpress.com
844-714-3454

Because of the dynamic nature of the Internet, any web addresses or links contained in this book may have changed since publication and may no longer be valid. The views expressed in this work are solely those of the author and do not necessarily reflect the views of the publisher, and the publisher hereby disclaims any responsibility for them.

Any people depicted in stock imagery provided by Getty Images are models, and such images are being used for illustrative purposes only. Certain stock imagery © Getty Images.

Scripture taken from the NEW AMERICAN STANDARD BIBLE®, Copyright © 1960, 1962, 1963, 1968, 1971, 1972, 1973, 1975, 1977, 1995 by The Lockman Foundation. Used by permission. www.Lockman.org

ISBN: 978-1-6642-2106-2 (sc)
ISBN: 978-1-6642-2105-5 (hc)
ISBN: 978-1-6642-2107-9 (e)

Library of Congress Control Number: 2021901292

Print information available on the last page.

WestBow Press rev. date: 02/19/2021

This Common Man's Commentary
is dedicated to my loving
wife Marie.

A special thanks to
Mark and Gina Stropkaj
and Nicholas and Pattie Cafaro,
for their support and encouragement
in making this Commentary possible.

Together,

We Stand Upon the Truth of God's Word, knowing

"Man shall not live on bread alone, but on every
word that proceeds out of the mouth of God"
(Matthew 4:4).

Therefore,

"Be diligent to present yourself approved to God
as a workman who does not need to be ashamed,
handling accurately the word of truth"
(2 Timothy 2:15).

TABLE OF CONTENTS

"But sanctify Christ as Lord in your hearts, always being ready to make a defense to everyone who asks you to give an account for the hope that is in you, yet with gentleness and reverence" (1 Peter 3:15).

INTRODUCTION
(OR OPENING ARGUMENT)

"Again, the kingdom of heaven is like a merchant
seeking fine pearls, and upon finding one
pearl of great value, he went and sold all that
he had and bought it" (Matthew 13:45, 46).

Opening Argument for this Commentary

The reason for doing this commentary, which ended up being over 50,000 words, started out as an effort to determine the 'day' of the week on which Jesus was crucified. Why is that important? Because for centuries theologians have been saying that Jesus died on what is known as "Good Friday."[1] For many it has been hard to accept this as the 'day,' when it should seem obvious that it could not have been on a Friday. For centuries the church may have been teaching something that is in error. With this thought in mind, there was a need to try and settle this question once and for all. This is necessary so that one may preach and teach about this subject with confidence and clarity. All would agree that the day and date are insignificant in comparison to the fact that Jesus Christ, as the Son of God, died on the cross as a sacrifice for our sins. What is of the utmost importance is receiving redemption by His blood shed for us, having our sins forgiven, and being given the gift of eternal life through faith in Him.

This is the true message of the New Testament, and Jesus as the Passover Lamb is what ties this together.

This will be an in depth look at the day of the crucifixion, and all the surrounding days that were part of that whole week. It will lead into the Old Testament establishment of Passover, its accompanying dates, and the requirements for its observance. How the day of Passover is determined and what are the demands of that day, and the surrounding days, will also be looked into. The challenge will be the deciphering of what the law required and what was practiced as tradition, for both are recorded. That whole week of Christ's passion will be laid out. It is possible to figure out the events of that week for the purpose of showing a timeline. Then there will be a closer look at the events of each day that surrounded the day of that Passover. The Scriptures themselves hold enough information to answer all questions on this matter.

Interspersed with these thoughts will be a look at the origination of the Passover lamb, and what the Bible says about its requirements. The Passover lamb is of course the main object of Passover and points us to Christ. One does not have to look far to realize that Jesus is the Passover Lamb sacrificed for us. With this in-depth study, a wonderful new door of understanding will open. As this study started out to show the day of the week of the crucifixion; it soon took on a larger scope of study with an inescapable conclusion. That conclusion has become the title of this study and a springboard for further studies. It will be shown that The Lamb is a progressive revelation in the Bible, from cover to cover. There is also the types and shadows, related to Passover and to the Lamb, which are satisfied and fulfilled by Jesus. At one time Jesus said He came not to destroy the law and prophets, but to fulfill. That He surely did, meeting all the requirements of the law and fulfilling all the reasons for His very coming. The importance that Scripture places on this Passover will then be shown by the revelation of the Lamb in heaven.

Jesus' death was more than a fulfillment of Passover but also of that which He Himself said while here on this earth. All the things that He and others said, like John the Baptist and the Apostle Paul, were under the inspiration of the Holy Spirit of God. Therefore, it had to be just as they had spoken. The whole of the gospel accounts builds up to the fulfillment of Passover, with Jesus as its Passover Lamb. Then the gospels end suddenly with only a few other pages concerning His resurrection and ascension. As great as these events were, they were without any great herald like at His first coming. This great heralding is awaiting His Second Coming.

Jesus would not die on just any day, but it had to be on the Day of Passover, even though the Jewish leaders <u>did not</u> want it to happen during the feast. For it is written: "Then the chief priests and the elders of the people were gathered together in the court of the high priest, named Caiaphas; and they plotted together to seize Jesus by stealth and kill Him. But they were saying, "Not during the festival, otherwise a riot might occur among the people" (Matthew 26:3-5; also, Mark 14:1, 2). God would have His way and carry out His purposes, and it would happen on this very Passover Day. God is not caught off guard on this Passover, nor was He on that day in Eden's garden when the deceiver did have his way. God would not take away the free-will of mankind, even to disobey, for He loved them too much. God had Himself a lamb, slain from the foundation of the world, waiting in the wings. The Lamb was to be revealed in the fullness of time, but until then only types and shadows of Him would be seen.

Another day would come when that same deceiver would play right into the hand of Him who created him. God would come in the flesh and offer Himself for His most precious creation, those created after His own likeness and in His image. Mankind would again have to use his free-will, this time to receive or reject the love that was made manifest to them. The stage was set, the day had come, it was Passover, and the hour would now be at hand.

This is The Story ... It is a LOVE STORY, and it is HIS-STORY (History).

Jesus Himself said many things about His death. Like, "And I, if I am lifted up from the earth, will draw all men to Myself," but He was saying this to indicate the kind of death by which He was to die" (John 12:32, 33). He also said, "Behold, we are going up to Jerusalem; and the Son of Man will be delivered to the chief priests and scribes, and they will condemn Him to death, and will hand Him over to the Gentiles to mock and scourge and crucify Him, and on the third day He will be raised up" (Matthew 20:18, 19). From this it is seen that He would be lifted up upon a pole, or tree, as Moses did in the wilderness, He would be crucified and die, and then be raised on the third day. He said, "Destroy this temple and in three days I will raise it up" - *meaning His body* - (John 2:19).

It becomes obvious that the day He died is especially important, as was the day He rose again. These were necessary for Jesus to be who He said He was and to fulfill all that He said. Jesus was destined to lay down His life on Passover, and now He must also rise again in three days. Tradition says Jesus died on a Friday, but there are those who say it was on Thursday, and still others say Wednesday. Any other views of different days are far and few between.

What do you say? To some it seems obvious, but that is easy to say. The problem is how does one prove their convictions? Most people have no concern about this issue, but those who are a student of the Word would like further understanding on this subject. There are countless articles that are written on this already, so why bother to write another? The answer is because it has to make sense! Especially if one is going to teach new believers. Believers are to be ready to give sensible answers to unbelievers as the Scriptures call us to do. For it is written:

- "Be diligent to present yourself approved to God, a worker who does not need to be ashamed, accurately handling the Word of Truth" (2 Timothy 2:15).
- "Preach the Word! Be ready in season and out of season. reprove, rebuke, exhort, with great patience and instruction" (2 Timothy 4:2).
- "But sanctify the Lord God in your hearts, always being ready to make a defense to everyone who asks you to give an account for the hope that is in you, yet with gentleness and reverence" (1 Peter 3:15).

Ok then, here is the stumbling block for this traditional view that one cannot ignore. It is… THE SIGN OF JONAH.

"For just as Jonah was three days and three nights in the belly of the sea monster, so will the Son of Man be three days and three nights in the heart of the earth" (Matthew 12:40).

Jesus made this statement about Jonah, but He was referring to His death, burial and resurrection that would be likewise. If this is true, and it must be true since Jesus said it, then there is no way for the normally accepted day of the crucifixion to be on a Friday. The reason Friday is the accepted day, is because they removed Jesus from the cross due to the Sabbath approaching at 6 p.m. The Sabbath being the seventh day of the Jewish week, or our Saturday, therefore, the day before had to be Friday. The day following the Sabbath was Sunday. The rationale is that the three days were Friday, Saturday, and Sunday, with Sunday being the third day.

The problem is there are not three days _and_ three nights between Friday and the morning of the first day of the week, which is Sunday, the accepted day of the resurrection.

The Scriptures are true and without error, and Jesus did not lie or get it wrong. So why do many, if not most, accept this religious belief or practice, which has become a tradition? If there are still unanswered questions on this, then one must search the Scriptures themselves, as done here. If further help is still needed one must look to honored historians and other reliable sources, but only if necessary, as was also done here. This is where this study will begin, knowing it is up against a lot of history, and a highly traditional way of thinking. This study will go against what seems to be the readily accepted answer. Acceptable, only if one does not really give much thought to it. But what about this one little verse concerning the sign of Jonah? It cannot be dismissed or overlooked. It is known that sometimes one must sift through a mountain of confusion to find a grain of truth. The work is hard, but the rewards are great. It is like finding that pearl of great price that Jesus talked about. To find and know the truth is to be set free from doubt and uncertainty. Once the truth is found it brings life and freedom.

It will be shown that Jesus did accomplish all that was required of Him to fulfill the Feast of Passover, and He fulfilled the sign of Jonah, as He said He would.

It is believed that Jesus' crucifixion, the Passover, the Passover Lamb, His burial and resurrection, and the sign of Jonah will all come together like pieces of a puzzle with this in-depth study. Again, to some this is no big deal, and some may even agree that it was a Thursday crucifixion. But Scripture must show it to be true! There are many statements made today about spiritual things and even preached as being so, but they are without any Scriptural insight or references given. Some will use one little verse as a major defense. Some take a verse and interpret it for you rather than letting the verse interpret itself. Still others take great liberties to make a verse or verses say what they want it to say. God forbid that would be the case here.

This study is also about the relevance of how these two subjects of the book's title are intertwined. It is not about some new revelation, for the truth has always been there. To find it though, one must take the time to dig into the Scriptures. Getting to the root of the truth is an exciting adventure, and it can lead to places that were never expected. That is what happened here. From a simple study of 'which day of the week' to the 'Fulfillment of Passover'! Wow, that is huge. John the Baptist said, "Behold the Lamb of God who takes away the sin of the world" (John 1:29). It is believed that those around him knew what John meant when he made that statement. It meant that the person he was addressing would be God's Lamb and the sacrifice for our sins. It was prophetic of Jesus' death as the Passover lamb sacrificed on the 14th of Nisan. The Apostle Paul confirms this when he said, "Christ our Passover also has been sacrificed" (1 Corinthians 5:7).

Not only do many celebrate "Good Friday," but think about all the yearly observances of Passover that still go on today. Although it is still a Jewish Feast Day, do Christians give any thought to its continued observance? Is it to go on forever? Read anything on the Passover, outside of the Bible, and it will say, "It is ..." and it will not say, "It was ..." So, the question is, "Did Jesus fulfill the Passover or not?"

*** When God put an end to offerings and sacrifices, through His Son's perfect offering and sacrifice, once, for all; did He mean for the practice of offering sacrifices to continue in any way? ***

Before you answer, think about this:

*** When God allowed the Roman armies to destroy His sacred temple and His beloved city of Jerusalem in 70 A.D.,[2] as Jesus forewarned, was He saying that He really meant it: NO MORE SACRIFICES FOR SIN? *** Not physically or spiritually.

This obviously included the sacrifice of the Passover lamb and its remembrance that is being replaced by Jesus' sacrifice once and for all. If so, then Passover is just that, it is over – having been fulfilled! "Samuel said, "Has the Lord as much delight in burnt offerings and sacrifices as in obeying the voice of the Lord? Behold, to obey is better than sacrifice, and to heed than the fat of rams. For rebellion is as the sin of divination, and insubordination is as iniquity and idolatry..." (1 Samuel 15:22, 23). David said, "For You do not delight in sacrifice, otherwise I would give it; You are not pleased with burnt offering. The sacrifices of God are a broken spirit; A broken and a contrite heart, O God, You will not despise" (Psalm 51:16, 17).

Come let us take this journey together and let the scriptures tell us what they have to say!

CHAPTER ONE

OLD TESTAMENT ACCOUNT
OF PASSOVER

"In the first month, on the fourteenth
day of the month at twilight is the
Lord's Passover" (Leviticus 23:5).

Establishing the Hebrew Month and Day of Passover

Before beginning a few facts will be gone over that will make the understanding of Passover easier, especially if one is not familiar with the Hebrew holy days. The Hebrew calendar year <u>ends</u> with what is called the '*tekufah*,'[1] which today is called the 'vernal equinox'. According to Merriam-Webster, '*Equinox*'[2] descends from '*aequus*,' the Latin word for 'equal,' and '*nox*,' the Latin word for 'night'. A fitting history for a word that describes days of the year when the daytime and nighttime are equal in length. In the northern hemisphere, the vernal equinox marks the first day of spring and occurs when the sun moves north across the equator. ('*Vernal*' comes from the Latin word '*ver*,' meaning 'spring.') The autumnal equinox marks the first day of autumn in the northern hemisphere and occurs when the sun crosses the equator going south. The Hebrew ecclesiastical calendar year <u>begins</u> with the first new moon appearance after the *tekufah*. That day becomes the first day of the first month. The fourteenth day of that month is Passover. For it is written: "In the first month, on the fourteenth day of the month at twilight is the Lord's Passover" (Leviticus 23:5).

Since the Hebrew month has either 29 or 30 days,[3] and Passover takes place on the fourteenth day of the month; it occurs when the moon is full, or almost full. This is because Passover is two weeks after the first appearance of the new moon. Scripture says, "Blow on the trumpet at the 'new moon' (*Hodesh*), at the 'full moon' (*Keseh*), and on our feast day" (Psalm 81:3). Passover[4] is the first of the annual holy days. Once its date is determined, it is simply a matter of counting days and months to set in place all the other Hebrew holy days. One may be surprised to learn that <u>Passover is not kept as a Sabbath</u>, for there is no Biblical command against work being done on it. In fact, there is much to do on that day.

Following the Passover, on the fourteenth, is the seven-day Feast of Unleavened Bread. This feast begins on the fifteenth day of the first month and ends on the twenty-first day. Both the first day and the last day of the Feast of Unleavened Bread are holy days of convocation, which mean they are High Sabbath days. It is written: "In the first month, on the fourteenth day of the month at twilight is the Lord's Passover. Then on the fifteenth day of the same month there is the Feast of Unleavened Bread to the Lord; for seven days you shall eat unleavened bread. On the first day you shall have a holy convocation (a High Sabbath); you shall not do any laborious work" (Leviticus 23:5-7).

The following two applicable scriptures were stated in the Introduction. First, John the Baptist said of Jesus, "Behold the Lamb of God who takes away the sin of the world" (John 1:29). He said this indicating who Jesus should be to them as a people, and eventually would be to the entire world. The Jews knew the significance of the Lamb of God. It was a reference to the lamb sacrificed, while in Egypt, in obedience to the Lord. The lamb's blood had to be applied to the door posts. When the Lord saw the blood, He passed over the houses of the children of Israel (Exodus 12:27). The blood of that lamb, shed for them, redeemed their lives. The second verse mentioned in the Introduction was the Apostle Paul saying, "Indeed Christ, our Passover also has been sacrificed" (1 Corinthians 5:7). This verse says and shows that our lives were redeemed in a like manner.

The establishing of Passover on the fourteenth of the month and the Feast of Unleavened Bread for the following seven days lead to the following conclusion: It was the fifteenth of Nisan, the first day of the Feast of Unleavened Bread, and a High Sabbath day, which was the approaching Sabbath and not the normal weekly seventh day Sabbath, which made it necessary to have Jesus removed from the cross.

The Old Testament Account of Passover

Here is what the Old Testament scriptures say about the Feast of Passover. "This month shall be the beginning of months for you; it is to be the first month of the year to you. Speak to all the congregation of Israel, saying, "On the tenth of this month they are each one to take a lamb for themselves, according to their fathers' households, a lamb for each household. Your lamb shall be an unblemished male a year old; you may take it from the sheep or from the goats. You shall keep it until the fourteenth day of the same month, then the whole assembly of the congregation of Israel is to kill it at twilight" (Exodus 12:2, 3, 5, 6). "Seven days you shall eat unleavened bread, but on the first day you shall remove leaven from your houses; for whoever eats anything leavened from the first day until the seventh day, that person shall be cut off from Israel. On the first day you shall have a holy assembly, and another holy assembly on the seventh day; no work at all shall be done on them, except what must be eaten by every person, that alone may be prepared by you" (Exodus 12:15, 16).

The Exodus account is verified in the Book of Leviticus. "In the first month, on the fourteenth day of the month at twilight is the Lord's Passover. Then on the fifteenth day of the same month there is the Feast of Unleavened Bread to the Lord; for seven days you shall eat unleavened bread. On the first day you shall have a holy convocation (a High Sabbath); you shall not do any laborious work. But for seven days you shall present an offering by fire to the Lord. On the seventh day is a holy convocation; you shall not do any laborious work" (Leviticus 23:5-8). This bears repeating, the fifteenth of Abib was the first day of the Feast of Unleavened Bread. It was a High Sabbath Day on which they did not do any manner of work, and they eat only unleavened bread.

The ecclesiastical calendar year started in the springtime, and Abib[5] was the first month of the new calendar year. These two parts of the Scripture (Exodus and Leviticus) tell us that they killed the Passover Lamb on the fourteenth day (of the first month- Abib), at twilight. The Israelite day is from 6 p.m. to 6 p.m., or sundown to sundown. This is based on the Genesis account of creation which says, "And there was evening and there was morning, one day" (Genesis 1:5b), and the second day etc. A verse in the Book of Judges best describes what a Jewish day is: "…Behold now, the day has drawn to a close; please spend the night. Lo, the day is coming to an end…" (Judges 19:9). Twilight on the fourteenth came at the end of the day, between 3 and 6 p.m., just prior to the start of a new day, the fifteenth, at evening. So, they killed Passover Lamb near the end of the day on the fourteenth of Abib.

They could do work on the fourteenth (Passover) which is also called the Preparation Day. That day is so named because of the preparation necessary for the Passover meal in the killing of the lamb, and the removal of any leaven from the house. The Passover meal was prepared during late day on the fourteenth, and eaten with unleavened bread, as evening approached. This carried over into the fifteenth of the month. For it is written: "You shall keep it (the Passover lamb) until the fourteenth day of the same month, then the whole assembly of the congregation of Israel is to kill it at twilight. In the first month, on the fourteenth day of the month at evening, you shall eat unleavened bread, until the twenty-first day of the month at evening" (Exodus 12:6, 18). None of the lamb's bones were to be broken for it was a type of Christ (Exodus 12:46, and John 19:36). It was to be consumed in haste because at the time in Egypt their deliverance was eminent. The meal was a remembrance that it came to pass at midnight the Lord struck the Egyptian firstborns, and He spared His people when He saw the blood over their door posts. It is believed that all of the Jewish faith has this understanding. For it is written: "...so you shall eat it in haste. It is the Lord's Passover. For I will go through the land of Egypt on that night and will strike down all the firstborn in the land of Egypt, both man and beast; and against all the gods of Egypt I will execute judgments- I am the Lord. And the blood shall be a sign for you on the houses where you live; and when I see the blood, I will pass over you, and no plague will befall you to destroy you when I strike the land of Egypt" (Exodus 12:11-13).

From Abib to Nisan

The Hebrew name of the first month was changed from Abib to Nisan.[6] Nisan was the word used in the times of the Mede and Persian Empire, whose king, Ahasuerus,[7] reigned from India to Ethiopia in the years 486 to 465 B.C. The Book of Esther mentions "...in the third year of his reign... (Esther 1:3), which would be 483 B.C. "In the first month, which is the month of Nisan..." (Esther 3:7). The Book of Nehemiah also refers to the new month of Nisan (Nehemiah 2, verse 1.) When the Israelites returned after their 70 years of Babylonian exile[8] they continued with the names of the Babylonian months. These names differ from the early Biblical months as you know. The New Testament does not refer to a month, only to the Passover and to the Feast of Unleavened Bread. What is known is that the first month of the new calendar year began in the Spring. This is today's March, or April, depending on when the vernal equinox occurs.

Jesus would become the Lamb of God who would redeem the children of God by His own blood shed upon a wooden post. This is carried out as the children of God take their Heavenly Father at His word, by faith. Like the faith Abraham showed in his own life and is referenced in the Book of Romans 4:20-22. It is especially important to remember what the prophet Habakkuk said, "...The righteous will live by his faith" (Habakkuk 2:4b).

What to Look Forward to

These seven statements will be presented in the following chapters, concerning the fulfillment of Passover and the timeline of the crucifixion, and shown there to be true:

#1. Jesus ate a meal on the Day of Passover.

#2. Jesus, as our Passover Lamb, was crucified on the fourteenth of Nisan, the fifth day of the Jewish week.

#3. Jesus was taken off the cross because at 6 p.m. the first of two consecutive Sabbaths were about to start.

#4. Jesus rose from the dead on the first day of the week.

#5. Jesus fulfills His own words and that of the prophets by rising from the dead after three days, on the first day of the week.

#6. Jesus fulfilled the requirements of the Passover Lamb, and so He fulfilled Passover also.

#7. The day of the crucifixion is the fifth day of the Jewish week, which would be our Thursday.

The following is the outline that will be adhered to in Chapters Two through Five, with the presupposition that Jesus died on the fourteenth of Nisan, the fifth day of the week (the Roman Thursday), as the Lord's Passover Lamb.

A. The Days Before the Passover- The eighth of Nisan until the thirteenth of Nisan (Passion Week[9]).

B. The Meal (Last Supper)- As the fourteenth of Nisan begins in the evening.

C. Return to the Garden of Gethsemane- After supper on the fourteenth of Nisan.

D. The Arrest and Events Before Dawn- Late evening until before 6 a.m. on the fourteenth of Nisan.

E. At the Cross and The Crucifixion- 9 a.m. on the fourteenth of Nisan, Passover day, until the end of day, before 6 p.m.

F. Events Following the Crucifixion- the fourteenth of Nisan until the seventeenth of Nisan (the first day of the week).

CHAPTER TWO

AN ACCOUNT OF THE 'PASSION WEEK' EVENTS

"…On the tenth of this month they are each one to take a lamb for themselves…" (Exodus 12:3).

Figure 1.
Month of Nisan, Hebrew Year 3795[1]

1st	2nd	3rd	4th	5th	6th	7th
					1	2
3	4	5	6	7	8	9
10	11	12	13	⟨14⟩	15	16
17	18	19	20	21	22	23
24	25	26	27	28	29	30

Figure 1.

The Passion Week[2]

This Chapter will follow the Hebrew Calendar of Figure 1 that gives the days and dates for the Hebrew month of Nisan, in the Hebrew year of 3795. This year on the Hebrew calendar corresponds to the Roman year 34 A.D. The calendar above is computer generated using official Hebrew dating and information courtesy of United States Naval Observatory Astronomical Applications Department.[3] The findings will be discussed in greater detail in Chapter Seven. The calendar of Figure 1 will act as a visual aid as the days of the week are being identified and discussed here.

A. The days before the Passover, starting six days prior

The 8th and the 9th of Nisan

Nisan 8, six days before Passover, the sixth day of the Jewish week.

"Jesus, therefore, six days before the Passover, came to Bethany where Lazarus was, whom Jesus had raised from the dead. So, they made Him a supper there, and Martha was serving; but Lazarus was one of those reclining at the table with Him" (John 12:1, 2).

Jesus is at Bethany six days before Passover. Therefore, the fourteenth, minus six, means it is the eighth of Nisan. He was at the house of Mary and Martha. Jesus stays for supper and now the night has become the seventh day of the week, and it is now the Sabbath at early evening.

Nisan 9, five days before Passover, the seventh day of the Jewish week.

"Mary then took a pound of very costly perfume of pure nard and anointed the feet of Jesus and wiped His feet with her hair; and the house was filled with the fragrance of the perfume. But Judas Iscariot, one of His disciples, who was intending to betray Him, said, "Why was this perfume not sold for three hundred denarii and given to poor people?" Now he said this, not because he was concerned about the poor, but because he was a thief, and as he had the money box, he used to pilfer what was put into it. Therefore, Jesus said, "Let her alone, so that she may keep it for the day of My burial" (John 12:3-7). That evening Mary anoints Jesus' feet with costly oil and dries them with her hair. A very similar event would happen two days before Passover at the house of Simon the leper.

This regular weekly Sabbath was the evening and the day. Traditionally individuals stayed at home like this and rested.

The 10ᵗʰ of Nisan

Nisan 10, four days before Passover, the first day of the Jewish week.

It was a day after the Sabbath, during the day, on the tenth. There was questionable money to be made on this day, as people had come from everywhere to prepare for the feast of Passover.

"On the next day the large crowd who had come to the feast, when they heard that Jesus was coming to Jerusalem, took the branches of the palm trees and went out to meet Him, and began to shout, "Hosanna! Blessed is He who comes in the name of the Lord, even the King of Israel." Jesus, finding a young donkey, sat on it; as it is written, "Fear not, daughter of Zion; behold, your King is coming, seated on a donkey's colt..." (John 12:12-15; also, Matthew 21:1-17; Mark 11:1-10; Luke 19:28-38; Zechariah 9:9). It was on the tenth of Nisan that the people of Israel had to 'take', or 'pick out,' or 'choose' for themselves, a lamb for each household, according to Exodus 12:3. Here, in this prophetic procession, is where we see Jesus chosen that day as both King and Lamb.

"When He had entered Jerusalem, all the city was stirred, saying, "Who is this?" And the crowds were saying, "This is the prophet Jesus, from Nazareth in Galilee." And Jesus entered the temple and drove out all those who were buying and selling in the temple and overturned the tables of the money changers and the seats of those who were selling doves. And He said to them, "It is written, "My house shall be called a house of prayer, but you are making it a robber's den" (Matthew 21:10-13), and (Isaiah 56:7). The buying of animals for the Passover sacrifice occurred on the tenth of Nisan. "Speak to all the congregation of Israel, saying, "On the tenth of this month they are each one to take a lamb for themselves, according to their fathers' households, a lamb for each household" (Exodus 12:3).

This practice had become shamefully dishonest, as implied by what Jesus did here prior to His last Passover. This was not the first time Jesus did this, for Jesus recognized this deceptive practice from the beginning. At the first Passover after His ministry began (John 2:13-15), Jesus made a whip of cords and overturned the tables and drove out the money changers. "And to those who were selling the doves, He said, "Take these things away; stop making My Father's house a place of busines." His disciples remembered that it was written, "Zeal for Your house will consume Me" (John 2:16-17) and (Psalm 69:9). Here Jesus says, "My Father's house," and in Matthew 21:10-13, He said, "My house," thus He can say in John 10:30, "I and My Father are one."

"And He was teaching daily in the temple. But the chief priests, and the scribes, and the leading men among the people were trying to destroy Him" (Luke 19:47). "And He left them and went out of the city to Bethany and spent the night there" (Matthew 21:17).

Note: If the tenth is the first day of the week, the fourteenth (Passover) is the fifth day.

The 11th thru the 13th of Nisan

Nisan 11, three days before Passover, the second day of the Jewish week.

"Now in the morning, when He was returning to the city, He became hungry. Seeing a lone fig tree by the road, He came to it and found nothing on it except leaves only; and He said to it, "No longer shall there ever be any fruit from you." And at once the fig tree withered. Seeing this, the disciples were amazed and asked, "How did the fig tree wither all at once" (Matthew 21:18-20)? "When He entered the temple, the chief priests and the elders of the people came to Him while He was teaching, and said, "By what authority are You doing these things, and who gave You this authority" (Matthew 21:23)? "When they sought to seize Him, they feared the people, because they (the people) considered Him to be a prophet" (Matthew 21:46). This day follows in context and is a day of teaching with all the challenges to those teachings.

Nisan 12, two days before Passover, the third day of the Jewish week.

"When Jesus had finished all these words, He said to His disciples, "You know that after two days the Passover is coming, and the Son of Man is to be handed over for crucifixion." Then the chief priests and the elders of the people were gathered in the court of the high priest, named Caiaphas; and they plotted together to seize Jesus by stealth and kill Him. But they were saying, "Not during the festival, otherwise a riot might occur among the people." Now when Jesus was in Bethany, at the home of Simon the leper, a woman came to Him with an alabaster vial of very costly perfume, and she poured it on His head as He reclined at the table" (Matthew 26:1-7). "For when she poured this perfume on My body, she did it to prepare Me for burial" (Matthew 26:12).

Mark also records the following. "Now the Passover and Unleavened Bread were two days away; and the chief priests and the scribes were seeking how to seize Him by stealth and kill Him" (Mark 14:1). This also shows in verse 3 that Jesus is at the house of Simon the leper. Matthew and Mark have both recorded that on this day Jesus was in Bethany at the <u>house of Simon the leper</u>, and a woman came to Him having an alabaster flask of very costly fragrant oil, and <u>she poured it on His head</u> as He sat at the table. Although the same costly oil is used and the same accusations are made, this is a different day for there is no mention of Mary, Martha, or Lazarus. Just like on the eighth day there is no mention of being at Simon the leper's house. Jesus says what this woman has done will be told as a memorial to her (Mark 14:3-9 and Matthew 26:6-13). Remembering that Judas was motivated by Satan, who is a thief and the accuser of the brethren (John 10:10a, and Revelation 12:10), and he would have influenced what this disciple had said.

Nisan 13, one day before Passover, the fourth day of the Jewish week.

"Now the Feast of Unleavened Bread, which is called the Passover was approaching. The chief priests and the scribes were seeking how they might put Him to death; for they were afraid of the people. And Satan entered into Judas who was called Iscariot, belonging to the number of the twelve. And he went away and discussed with the chief priests and officers how he might betray Him to them" (Luke 22:1-4).

"and (Judas) said, "What are you willing to give me to betray Him to you?" And they weighed out thirty pieces of silver to him" (Matthew 26:15).

"They were glad and agreed to give him money. So, he consented and began seeking a good opportunity to betray Him to them apart from the crowd" (Luke 22:5, 6).

Although it does not specifically say 'one day' before Passover, this is most probably the day. It must be assumed that Jesus was about doing His usual routine as mentioned earlier. "Now during the day, He was teaching in the temple, but at evening He would go out and spend the night on the Mount that is called Olivet. And all the people would get up early in the morning to come to Him in the temple to listen to Him" (Luke 21:37, 38). As mentioned, Judas was very busy this day and must have left the disciples for a while to do what he did. This day was a very dark day in history; it was a day of betrayal. Tomorrow Jesus would say, "Judas, are you betraying the Son of Man with a kiss" (Luke 22:48)? This day would precede a much, much darker day than any had ever known. A day that would become the center of all history. History will show that those of the past would have looked forward to this day, and those who lived after this day would be looking back. It would be a Day of Redemption, but at a great, great price.

John the Baptist's words, "Behold, the Lamb of God who takes away the sin of the world" (John 1:29), would soon be fulfilled whereby Jesus ended up laying down His life.

CHAPTER THREE

FROM THE LAST SUPPER
TO THE LOST DISCIPLE

"Now when evening came, Jesus was reclining at
the table with the twelve disciples" (Matthew 26:20).

Nisan 14, (Preparation Day) Passover, the fifth day of the Jewish week.

Nisan 14 – The Place

6 p.m. - " Now on the first day of Unleavened Bread the disciples
came to Jesus and asked, "Where do You want us to prepare for You
to eat the Passover" (Matthew 26:17; also, Mark 14:12; Luke 22:7-9)?

This is now Passover, the first day of unleavened bread, when
they kill the Passover Lamb. It is the beginning of the fourteenth of
Nisan, early evening. It should be obvious that the Preparation Day
needed just that, preparations. The first question that this group of
wondering, but faithful few, would ask is "where do you want us to
prepare for you to eat the Passover" (i.e., we need a place)? It was
supper time on the evening of Nisan 14, which comes before the
daytime, and the disciples would need to prepare this supper meal.
They had no idea there would not be a Passover Meal to prepare
for the Master, nor for them. It was the early evening meal at the
beginning of the day, at evening time. This meal would consist of

bread (unleavened) and wine. It was not the same meal prepared with lamb for the next evening on the fourteenth, carrying over into the fifteenth. The disciples did just as Jesus had directed them; they found a place and they prepared for the Passover (Luke 22:9-13). First there would be a supper meal, but there would not be a traditional Passover meal for the disciples this year.

There may seem to be a few contradictions in the verse above (Matthew 26:17). Mainly, how can it be the first day of the Feast of Unleavened Bread and the Passover also? It has been said that the Passover, at this time in history, was now considered part of the Feast of Unleavened Bread. It appears to have become common practice to interchange the two commonly used terms, 'Passover' and 'Feast of Unleavened Bread,' for the seven or eight-day period.

Some even quote the historian Josephus[1] referring to this same predicament, as acceptable for the day. This is all confirmed in the New Testament in Luke 22:1, which says, "Now the Feast of Unleavened Bread, which is called Passover, was approaching." Also, Luke 22:7, which says, "Then came the first day of Unleavened Bread, on which the Passover lamb had to be sacrificed."

As one rereads this verse, it becomes clear that there really is no contradiction at all. First, one must realize it is now the beginning of the fourteenth of Nisan in the evening, when the fifth day of the week has just begun. These verses, Matthew 26:17, along with Mark 14:12 and Luke 22:7, in the Greek, do NOT say, "On the first day of the 'Feast' of Unleavened Bread..." (as is written in the King James Version, and the New King James Version). What it does say in the Greek is, "On the first day of unleavened bread in which the Passover lamb had to be sacrificed." From this we know it was the fourteenth and not the fifteenth. Remember, the fourteenth is also the first day that there is no leavened bread, according to Exodus 12:18, (See Chapter One). Passover is the first day when there is unleavened bread, and it is the day the lamb is sacrificed, as Luke 22:7 says.

That is all there is to it; it is the Day of Preparation, which the Passover is also known as. The Feast of Unleavened Bread still starts on the next day, the fifteenth, and it is a High Sabbath day. It bears repeating, the Feast of Unleavened Bread starts on the fifteenth of Nisan and it lasts until the twenty-first of Nisan. Remember unleavened bread is to be eaten all eight days of the feast, from the fourteenth to the twenty-first.

Nisan 14 – The Meal (The Last Supper)

"Now when evening came, Jesus was reclining at the table with the twelve disciples" (Matthew 26:20). "While they were eating, Jesus took some bread, and after a blessing, He broke it and gave it to the disciples, and said, "Take, eat; this is My body." And when He had taken a cup and given thanks, He gave it to them, saying, "Drink from it, all of you; for this is My blood of the covenant, which is poured out for many for forgiveness of sins. But I say to you, I will not drink of this fruit of the vine from now on until that day when I drink it new with you in My Father's kingdom" (Matthew 26:26-29; also, Mark 14:18-25; Luke 22:15-22; John 13:21-26).

On this day there was a *place* to prepare for the Passover, but there is no mention of a lamb at the meal. That is because of three reasons. One, they would not kill the Passover lamb for another twenty hours, or so, during the light of day. It was still early on the fourteenth in the evening hours of Passover. Second, because Jesus had spent hours, or days, telling His disciples that He, Himself, was the true Passover Lamb of God. He would also tell them that the bread stood for His body, and the wine His blood. Third, was because God was doing something new.

This meal that they had in the evening of Passover, before the day, was 'supper' and it consisted of bread and wine. It would become the new memorial meal. "Jesus said to them, "Truly, truly, I say to you, unless you eat the flesh of the Son of Man and drink

His blood, you have no life in yourselves" (John 6:53). What Jesus had used to give reference to Himself is found in its entirety in John 6:32-59. What we have instituted here is the Lord's Supper, or what is known as *Communion*.[2] (See 1 Corinthians 11:20-30). The Apostle Paul brings us into that room on that very night when he said: "For I received from the Lord that which I also delivered to you, that the Lord Jesus, on the night in which He was betrayed took bread; and when He had given thanks, He broke it and said, 'This is My body which is for you; do this in remembrance of Me. In the same way He took the cup also after supper, saying, "This cup is the new covenant in My blood; do this, as often as you drink it, in remembrance of Me" (1 Corinthians 11:23-25).

When Jesus began His ministry, it was completely different from anything the people had ever known. "The officers answered, "Never has a man spoken the way this man speaks" (John 7:46). They accused Him of many things, such as eating with sinners, doing work on the Sabbath, and possibly the worst thing, -speaking against the religious elite, just to mention a few. His sermon on the mount was like nothing they had ever heard. Jesus would say, "You have heard it said...<u>but I tell you...</u>" (Matthew 5:27, 28). This is not to say that Jesus did not live under and according to the law, for He did, having yet to fulfill it.

He told of a new covenant[3] of love and liberty, for His plan was to fulfill the old covenant[4] and then set up a new one. His disciples would become new creations to live and walk-in newness of life. Circumcision would not matter, neither would the place of worship. He would fulfill the Feast of Passover as the Passover Lamb, and He would reinstitute a new meal of remembrance. This meal is not a remembrance of deliverance from Egyptian bondage, but one from the enslavement of the Dominion of Sin. The communion meal is to be celebrated as often as the local body chooses, not just once a year. By it one remembers the life that Jesus laid down as a ransom payment for our sins. One would also remember the blood that He

FROM THE LAST SUPPER TO THE LOST DISCIPLE

shed for the remission of our sins; for without the shedding of blood there is no forgiveness of sin. As the Lamb of God, it would be His body that He gave and His blood that He had shed. This would now become the emphasis of the new meal. It was exactly as Jesus told them and as recorded in the earlier scripture from Matthew 26:26-29.

Jesus' life was without sin therefore He would be the only acceptable sacrifice for sin, once and for all. Hence the Passover meal is superseded by the communion meal, it is a reminder of the finished work of Christ. The believer would do this in remembrance of Him until He comes again. After His death on the cross there would no longer be any other acceptable sacrifice for sin. Then there would no longer be a need for the priesthood. Christ would become our great high priest, who entered the very presence of God. The veil would be torn in two and the believer would be able to come boldly before His throne of grace. It is written: "And He who sits on the throne said, "Behold, I am making all things new." And He said, "Write, for these words are faithful and true" (Revelation 21:5). This communion meal would just be the beginning, and it would certainly touch all areas of religious life, as was just mentioned.

Nisan 14 – The Betrayal

"Now before the Feast of the Passover, Jesus knowing that His hour had come that He should depart out of this world to the Father, having loved His own who were in the world, He loved them to the end. And during supper, the devil having already put it into the heart of Judas Iscariot, the son of Simon, to betray Him" (John 13;1, 2).

This verse is not saying a day before the Passover. It is saying 'before' the Feast of Passover, which is the festive 'meal' that is eaten after they kill the lamb. The people would all partake of this feast following the upcoming daylight hours beginning at twilight. That is when they enjoyed the feast of the Passover meal. What they had just eaten was a supper meal of bread and wine. After this Jesus rose and washed the disciple's feet (John 13:4-17). He told them that one of them would betray Him (John 13:18, 21, 26). "...Truly, truly, I say to you, that one of you will betray Me." "...That is the one for whom I shall dip the morsel and give it to him. After the morsel, Satan then entered into him. Therefore, Jesus said to him, "What you do, do quickly" (John 13:21, 26, 27). When the 'lost disciple' (Judas) had gone out, Jesus expounded on the following things to the eleven:

Jesus is the only way to the Father, and one with the Father.
(John Chapter 14.)
Jesus' command to love one another, and to bear much fruit.
(John Chapter 15.)
Jesus' promise to send the Helper, the Spirit of Truth.
(John Chapter 16.)
Jesus' intercessory prayer for His disciples, and for us.
(John Chapter 17.)

<u>Fact #1. Here Jesus eats a meal on the day of Passover in the early evening. This shows the answer of the first fact in Chapter One that states this very thing.</u>

"Fixing our eyes on Jesus, the author and perfecter of faith, <u>who for the joy</u> set before Him endured the cross, despising the shame, and has sat down at the right hand of the throne of God" (Hebrews 12:2).

CHAPTER FOUR

FROM THE GARDEN TO THE GRAVE

"…What shall I say, "Father, save Me
from this hour?" But for this purpose, I
came to this hour…" (John 12:27).

Nisan 14 – The Garden (of Gethsemane) Prayer

"When Jesus had spoken these words, He went forth with His disciples over the ravine of the Kidron, where there was a garden, in which He entered with His disciples" (John 18:1).

~9 p.m. – And when they had sung a hymn, they went out to the Mount of Olives.

"Then Jesus came with them to a place called Gethsemane, and said to the disciples, "Sit here while I go and pray over there." And He took with Him Peter and the two sons of Zebedee (James and John, Mark 3:17) and He began to be grieved and distressed" (Matthew 26:36, 37; also, Mark 14:32, 33). Jesus also said to them, "Pray that you may not enter into temptation" (Luke 22:40; also, Matthew 26:41; Mark 14:38). Jesus surely would be hard pressed, for He was in great spiritual warfare (Matthew 26:30-46; Mark 14:26-42; Luke 22:39-46).

The garden prayer is being looked at in depth here in order to help us understand what was meant by the words Jesus' spoke. It is always necessary <u>not</u> to take sayings out of context, and the context must be consistent with other Scriptures and their context of the same topic. Here is Jesus' prayer: **"Father, if you are willing, remove this cup from Me; yet not My will, but Yours be done"** (Luke 22:42; also, Matthew 22:39-44; Mark 14:36).

For most Christians, the meaning may seem to be obvious. Jesus in His humanity, as the Son of Man, did not want to endure the agony of the cross. He wanted God's will done and not His own, regardless of any natural human desires. Because Jesus asked that not His will be done but God's will, confirms this view for those who hold such a view. The following verses make mention of Jesus being made in human likeness. "Have this attitude in yourselves which was also in Christ Jesus, who, although He existed in the form of God, did not regard equality with God a thing to be grasped, but emptied Himself, taking the form of a bond-servant, and being made in the likeness of men" (Philippians 2:5-7).

Is it possible for there to be any other answer for Jesus asking for this cup to be removed from Him? And what is the 'cup' that Jesus is asking to be removed? Is it the suffering of the cross before Him, or could it be something else?

The three questions that need to be asked are these:

Q1. What is the cup that Jesus is referring to?
Q2. Why is He asking for this cup to be taken away?
Q3. Why did Jesus think His will may be different?

Q1. A 'cup' is a metaphor for trials or suffering. "This cup is the new covenant in My blood" (1 Corinthians 11:25). The cup that would require the shedding of His blood and the giving of His life. Another place that a 'cup' is mentioned is when Jesus' disciples, James and John, ask Him to grant their request.

"They said to Him, "Grant that we may sit, one on Your right and one on Your left, in Your glory." But Jesus said to them, "You do not know what you are asking. Are you able to drink the cup that I drink, or to be baptized with the baptism with which I am baptized?" They said to Him, "We are able." And Jesus said to them, "The cup that I drink you shall drink; and you shall be baptized with the baptism with which I am baptized. But to sit on My right or on My left, this is not Mine to give; but it is for those for whom it has been prepared" (Mark 10:37-40).

It sounds like He is asking them if they can go through what He knows He will have to go through, which may also include the giving of their lives. The Apostle Paul declares for himself: "that I may know Him and the power of His resurrection and the 'fellowship of His sufferings', being conformed to His death" (Philippians 3:10). Here the fellowship of His suffering seems to be referring to 'the same cup.' Remember they successfully martyred all the disciples for their faith in Christ, except for John.

Q2. Why would Jesus be asking for this cup of suffering to pass from Him? Would it be His humanity or is something else going on? Jesus had one mission and purpose from the very beginning and that was to give His life as a ransom for many (Matthew 20:28; Mark 10:45; John 13:1-17). This He knew, and to this one end He was committed. The following was recorded early in Jesus' ministry: "But He warned them and instructed them to not tell this to anyone, saying, "The Son of Man must suffer many things, and be rejected by the elders and chief priests and scribes, <u>and be killed</u> and be raised the third day" (Luke 9:21, 22).

Regardless of this knowledge, and also because of this knowledge, Jesus never flinched. "When the days were approaching for His ascension, <u>He was determined</u> to go to Jerusalem" (Luke 9:51). This fulfilled what Isaiah the prophet said, "For the Lord GOD helps Me; Therefore, I am not disgraced; Therefore, <u>I have set My face like a flint,</u> and I know that I will not be ashamed" (Isaiah 50:7).

Jesus was resolute in His determination to face what was before Him at Jerusalem, knowing that the Lord God, His Father would help Him. Also knowing that there was no way He would end up disgraced nor ashamed. Again, this is contrary to what is the popular belief.

He also knew when His hour had come, "Now before the Feast of the Passover, Jesus <u>knowing</u> that His hour had come that He should depart from this world to the Father..." (John 13:1). Knowing when His hour had come Jesus did not pray that it would pass, because He knew He was going to the Father. Why would He ask for it to pass? We never see Jesus being afraid of anything, not storms, not demons, and not beatings nor pain. In fact, Jesus confirms this shortly afterwards while still in the garden, when it says, "So Jesus said to Peter, "Put the sword into the sheath; <u>the cup </u>which the Father has given Me, <u>shall I not drink it</u>" (John 18:11)? He was not asking for the cup of the suffering of the cross to be removed – no, not at all.

It was Jesus' will to drink the cup the Father had given Him.

Do not forget this: "Fixing our eyes on Jesus, the author and perfecter of faith, <u>who for the joy</u> set before Him endured the cross, despising the shame, and has sat down at the right hand of the throne of God" (Hebrews 12:2).

There was no fear or weakness of humanity here, quite the opposite. It was for the <u>joy set before Him</u> that Jesus was looking forward to, and willing to, endured the cross. No one was taking His life from Him; He was laying it down of His own free will (John 10:18). Why then did Jesus ask for the cup to be removed? It cannot be denied that as Jesus prayed, He was in great agony and sorrowful unto death. His sweat became like great drops of blood, even as He was falling on His face!

It may have been that Jesus thought that He might die before He had a chance to go to the cross. He surely felt that way because of the *'great agony'* that He was going through physically. Could this be what He was asking would pass; that He not die now, and have a chance to go to the cross to bear the sins of the world? The Father may have had something else in mind, and if so, Jesus would defer His will to the Father's will. "Not MY will but Yours be done." This is what the Scriptures say of Jesus' physical condition, <u>even after</u> the angels had come and ministered to Him: "And being in agony, He prayed very fervently; and His sweat became like great drops of blood falling down upon the ground" (Luke 22:44).

This is a known medical condition as found in the Indian Journal of Dermatology: Hematohidrosis[1], which is also known as Hematidrosis, hemidrosis and hematidrosis, is a condition in which capillary blood vessels that feed the sweat glands rupture, causing them to exude blood, occurring under conditions of <u>extreme</u> physical or emotional stress. Hematohidrosis is a rare clinical condition of sweating blood and it may occur when a person is suffering from extreme stress; for example, facing his or her own death.

At this time Jesus is under extreme emotional stress and temptation like no other. Speaking directly to His disciples: (Jesus) "said to them, 'My soul is <u>deeply grieved</u>, <u>to the point of death</u>; remain here and keep watch with Me.' And He went a little beyond them and fell on His face..." (Matthew 26:38, 39). Can this at least be a consideration, if not the actual reasoning for this prayer! "The spirit is indeed willing but, the flesh is weak," just as Jesus said to His disciples during this time (Matthew 26:41). Jesus prays these words three times according to Matthew's account (Matthew 26:44), because it was not passing, and was so very, very real.

Q3. This could also be the reasoning why Jesus thought He had to defer to the Father's will. Jesus was willing to endure the sufferings of the cross and believed it was the Father's will for Him, for they always agreed. Because Jesus physically felt that He might die, or at least not make it to the cross; Jesus earnestly prayed that this would pass. The accompanying feelings & thoughts were very real but so was the hope that He would still be able to go to the cross. But if the Father's will be somehow different, then He would willingly submit Himself.

Jesus' will is always the same as the Father's, and up until now there was no reason to think any differently. The Bible says, "Therefore Jesus answered and was saying to them, "Truly, truly, I say to you, the Son can do nothing of Himself, unless it is something He sees the Father doing; for whatever the Father does, these things the Son also does in like manner. For the Father loves the Son and shows Him all things that He Himself is doing; and the Father will show Him greater works than these, so that you will marvel" (John 5:19, 20).

Earlier in the week Jesus had said, "Now My soul has become troubled; and <u>what shall I say, "Father, save Me from this hour?" But for this purpose, I came to this hour</u>. Father glorify Your name. Then a voice came from heaven, saying, "I have both glorified it and will glorify it again" (John 12:27, 28). Here Jesus tells us Himself that He <u>would not</u> ask the Father to save Him from this hour, for this is the purpose of His coming. Therefore, it was for another reason as we surmised. Jesus had angels come minister to Him after being forty days in the wilderness tempted by the devil and not eating. Now Jesus needs ministry from the angels again for both physical and spiritual reasons, as He is now going through this very real temptation.

<u>Not</u> because He did not want to go to the cross! That is absurd! Jesus was fully aware, and knew then, as always, that He was the Passover Lamb. The Lamb who would take away the sins of the world (John 1:29); and that He was the Lamb slain from the foundation of the world (Revelation 13:8). Speaking of the foundation of the world, Jesus said these words just prior to going to the garden. "Father, I desire (will) that they also whom You have given Me, be with Me where I am, so that they may see My glory which You have given Me, for You loved Me, before the foundation of the world" (John 17:24).

Just moments before crossing over the Brook Kidron Jesus prays to the Father, that those whom the Father has given to Him may be where He is and behold His glory. Jesus knows the only way this can happen is if He goes to the cross and bears their sins. He cannot save Himself because His desire and will is to save those who the Father has given Him. No, He would never pray that the cup, the suffering of the cross, be removed from Him. No never! But He would pray that the cup of suffering, that would keep Him from going to the cross, be removed! It was Jesus' will that they (His disciples and all future believers) be with Him and behold the glory the Father has given Him before the foundation of the world, - BECAUSE THE FATHER LOVES HIM.

It is also interesting to note that we, as the 'church,' spend so much time trying to justify with our own human reasoning, why Jesus said this. The Apostle John recorded four chapters that gave every detail to what happened during and after the last supper. He included the long prayers but gave no mention whatsoever to this one-line prayer in the garden. John just goes from them crossing the brook into the garden, to Judas' betrayal, <u>and he was there</u>! Earlier in John's gospel Jesus said to His disciples, "My food is to do the will of Him who sent Me, and to accomplish His work" (John 4:34). And again, "Jesus, knowing that the Father had given all things into His hands, and that He had come forth from God and was going back to God" (John 13:3). He knew what He had to do, and it was His will to do it. This really should settle this controversy.

Nisan 14 – The Arrest and Events Before Dawn

~12 a.m. – And Judas, who betrayed Him, also knew the place: for Jesus often met there with His disciples.

- Judas came with a great multitude from the chief priests and elders having both swords and staves.

- Jesus was betrayed with a kiss.
- Peter cuts off the ear of the high priest's servant, which Jesus heals.
- All the disciples fled.

(Matthew 26:47-56; Mark 14:42-50; Luke 22:47-53; John 18:3-11)
~3 a.m. – Jesus was bound and sent to Annas and then to Caiaphas the high priest.

- Peter denies Jesus three times.
- Jesus blindfolded, spit upon, mocked and beaten.

(John 18:12-27; Matthew 26:57-75; Mark 14:53-72; Luke 22:54-65)
~6 a.m. – Early morning (on the 14th) Jesus was sent from Caiaphas to Pilate, the governor.

- The Jews did not go into the Praetorium, so that they would not be defiled and be able to eat the Passover (John 18:28).
- Pilate finds no fault in Him.
- Learning He is a Galilean; Pilate sends Jesus to Herod.
- Herod and his men mock Jesus and put a robe on Him.
- Herod sends Jesus back to Pilate.
- Pilate wanted to release Jesus.
- The people cried out for Barabbas to be released.
- They also cried out for Jesus to be crucified and prevailed.
- Jesus was scourged and received a crown of thorns.
- Jesus was spit upon and hit on the head.
- Mocking they said "Hail, King of the Jews"
- It was the Day of Preparation, the Passover, about the sixth hour when they said, "Behold your King."
- Simon of Cyrene was made to bear His cross, following from behind.
- They came to Golgotha, which means the Place of the Skull.

(John 18:28 to John 19:17; Matthew 27:1-33; Mark 15:1-22; Luke 22:66 to Luke 23:32)

Note: Only the Gospel of John uses Roman time with the day beginning at 12 a.m. The sixth hour of the Roman day is 6 a.m.

Nisan 14 – At the Cross and the Crucifixion

9 a.m. – Now it was the third hour (9 a.m. Jewish time), and they crucified Jesus (Mark 15:25).

- They nailed Jesus' hands and feet to the cross (John 20:25-27; Psalm 22:16).
- They gave Jesus sour wine mixed with gall to drink (Psalm 22:15).
- Jesus was crucified between two robbers.
- The sign placed over His head said, "Jesus of Nazareth King of the Jews."
- The soldiers cast lots for His garments (Psalm 22:18).
- Jesus was blasphemed and mocked by those passing by (Psalm 22:6-8).

(John 19:18-29; Matthew 27:34-44; Mark 15:23-32; Luke 23;33-43)

Note: The Jewish day begins at 6 a.m. with the third hour of the Jewish day being 9 a.m.

Nisan 14 – Darkness Over the Whole Land

12 noon till 3 p.m. – It was now about the sixth hour, (12 noon) and darkness fell over the whole land until the ninth hour, (3 p.m.), (Luke 23:44; Matthew 27:45; Mark 15:33).

There was darkness over the whole land, some say all the earth. The whole world may have experienced the darkness of that day, and most without any awareness of the great price that was being paid for their sin. Do we today understand what He did for us then? The ransom was paid in full.

Nisan 14 – The Moment of Christ's Death

3 p.m. – And at the ninth hour (3 p.m.) Jesus cried out with a loud voice (Mark 15:34).

- Jesus cried out again, "I thirst," and finally "It is finished."
- Jesus gave up His Spirit.
- The veil in the temple tore in two from top to bottom.
- The earth quaked, rocks split apart, and graves were opened.

(John 19:30-42; Matthew 27:50-56; Mark 15:34-41; Luke 23:44-54)

The 14ᵗʰ – After the Crucifixion at the End of Day

"Then the Jews, because it was the day of preparation, so that the bodies would not remain on the cross on the Sabbath (for that Sabbath was a high day), asked Pilate that their legs might be broken, and that they might be taken away" (John 19:31).

"But when they came to Jesus and saw that He was already dead, they did not break His legs. Instead, one of the soldiers pierced His side with a spear, and immediately blood and water flowed out" (John 19:34, 35).

- It was early evening as the Sabbaths drew near on the Day of Preparation.
- Jesus was already dead, so they did not break His legs (Reference is Exodus 12:36).
- They pierced His side with a spear, water and blood flow out.
- Joseph of Arimathea asked Pilate for the body of Jesus (John 19:38).

- Nicodemus came bringing about a 100 pounds of a mixture of myrrh and aloes (John 19:39).
- They took the body of Jesus and wrapped it in strips of linen with the spices (John 19:40).
- They placed Jesus in a new tomb where no one ever laid (John 19:41).
- Mary Magdalene and the other Mary sat opposite the tomb (Matthew 27:61).

Nisan 14 –The Day is Done, but The Story is Only Half Over

Jesus Christ was crucified and died on Passover, the 14th of Nisan at 3 p.m. It is the fifth day of the Jewish week, as the day now draws to a close. They had placed Jesus' body in the tomb some time before. Jesus' burial was still during the day-time hours on this special (fifth day) Thursday. This would begin the first day of the three days and three nights according to the sign of Jonah. The new day drawing near was a High Sabbath Day for it would be the fifteenth of Nisan at evening, the first day of the Feast of Unleavened Bread.

The verse which says, "that Sabbath was a High Day" (John 19:31), confirms this. Clearly this means it was not the normal weekly Sabbath that fell on the seventh day of the Jewish week. This was the first of the two consecutive Sabbaths that week. It was the approaching evening that would start the High Sabbath at 6 p.m. That evening would be the first night of the three days and three nights according to the sign of Jonah. The sign of Jonah will be discussed in greater detail in later chapters.

Fact #2 & #3. Here Jesus is definitely crucified on the 14th of Nisan, the fifth day of the week. He was taken off the cross because the first of two consecutive Sabbaths was approaching on the fifteenth, the sixth day of the Jewish week.

THE LAMB has been Slain.

There is no more Sacrifice for Sin.

"...For Christ our Passover also has been sacrificed"
(1 Corinthians 5:7).

Next is an account of the events that followed the crucifixion.

CHAPTER FIVE

AN ACCOUNT OF EVENTS AFTER CHRIST'S CRUCIFIXION

"For as yet they did not understand the Scripture,
that He must rise again from the dead" (John 20:9).

The 14th through the 18th of Nisan

Nisan 14, - after the Crucifixion, still the fifth day of the Jewish week.

Before Jesus would rise bodily, His Spirit would first descend to Abraham's Bosom.[1] Abraham's Bosom is a portion of 'Hades,' where the spirits and souls of the righteous dead were held. Hades is the Old Testament 'Sheol.' This is the place talked about in the story of the rich man and Lazarus found in Luke Chapter Sixteen.

The Psalmist said about Jesus, "For You will not abandon my soul to Sheol; Nor will You allow Your Holy One to undergo decay" (Psalm 16:10). To undergo decay is as to not 'see corruption,' as mentioned elsewhere. Meaning that His body would not be in the ground long enough to decay, which would be longer than three days. That is the natural course of events. One should remember at the death of Lazarus: "Jesus said, "Remove the stone." Martha, the sister of the deceased, said to Him, "Lord, by this time there is a stench, for he has been dead four days" (John 11:39).

The Palmist also said, "You have ascended on high, You have

led captive Your captives; You have received gifts among men, even among the rebellious also, that the Lord God may dwell there" (Psalm 68:18).

The Apostle Paul quotes this in part in his famous letter to the Ephesians, "Therefore it says: When He ascended on high, He led captive a host of captives, And He gave gifts to men." But then Paul went on to say, "(Now this expression, 'He ascended,' what does it mean except that He also had descended into the lower parts of the earth? He who descended is Himself also He who ascended far above all the heavens, so that He might fill all things.) And He gave some to be apostles, some prophets..." (Ephesians 4:8-11).

Peter picks up on this by saying, "For Christ also died for sins once for all, the just for the unjust, so that He might bring us to God, having been put to death in the flesh, but made alive in the spirit; in which also He went and made proclamation to the spirits now in prison, who once were disobedient, when the patience of God kept waiting in the days of Noah, during the construction of the ark, in which a few, that is, eight persons, were brought safely through the water" (1 Peter 3:18-20).

Jesus was buried (put in the tomb) near the end of the day before evening came. Therefore, for any part of the next three days and three nights He descends to where the spirits and souls of the departed were in Hades. (Again, see the story of the rich man and Lazarus, Luke 16:19-31.)

Nisan 15 - one day after Passover, the sixth day of the Jewish week.

This is the first day of the Feast of Unleavened Bread, a High Sabbath day. A High Sabbath, and also the first of two approaching Sabbaths, as mentioned in John 19:31. Again, the 'evening' of the fifteenth, comes before the 'day' of the fifteenth. This day was a high holy day and these religious leaders were active instead of resting and worshipping. The scriptures say,

Now on the next day, the day after the preparation, the chief priests and the Pharisees gathered together with Pilate, and said, "Sir, we remember that when He was still alive that deceiver said, "After three days I am to rise again." Therefore, give orders for the grave to be made secure until the third day, otherwise His disciples may come and steal Him away and say to the people, "He has risen from the dead," and the last deception will be worse than the first. Pilate said to them, "You have a guard; go, make it as secure as you know how." And they went and made the grave secure, and along with the guard they set a seal on the stone" (Matthew 27:62-66).

This idea of securing the tomb until the third day, with this already being the first day, does not seem to make sense. For they even said that Jesus said, "after three days I am to rise again." This thought about the third day is to be looked at later in this chapter.

Jesus' body is now in the tomb, and His Spirit has descended into Hades. He is there to preach to the captives that He is the One they have been longing and waiting for. The One for whom Abraham had lived by faith. The One to whom Noah was a preacher of righteousness. The One who was the Promised Seed, the Rock in the Wilderness, the Son of David, the Anointed One, the Messiah, and the Son of God.

Nisan 16, - two days after Passover, the seventh day of the Jewish week.

This was the second day of the Feast of Unleavened Bread, the normal weekly Sabbath. It is believed that it was during this day that the women prepared the spices. "Then they returned and prepared spices and perfumes" (Luke 23:56a). Although it sounds like the same day or shortly thereafter, they knew Nicodemus had properly prepared the body. They were there and saw it, so what they were doing was preparing for the first day of the week. The guards had secured the tomb and the stone was already in place. It is written: "See, the Lord has given you the sabbath; therefore, He gives you bread for two days on the sixth day. Remain every man in his place; let no man go out of his place on the seventh day." So, the people rested on the seventh day" (Exodus 16:29, 30).

In the days in which Jesus lived, it was different from when the command was given in the time of the Exodus. There were synagogues[2] in many of the Jewish towns. They were called the "Place of Gathering"—*Beit Kenesset* in Hebrew, or *'synagogos'* in Greek. The purpose of the synagogue was to provide a place of communal prayer. The Temple in Jerusalem was the primary public place of worship for the Jews up until the Romans destroyed the Second Temple in 70 A.D. The synagogue is now the only place for public worship and keeps reaching increased importance over the years.

One cannot but imagine how things were on that Sabbath, although we have nothing recorded for that day. Prior to this week Jesus was constantly in the synagogue on the Sabbath, or He was at the Temple, and doing things that were quite unorthodox according to Jewish tradition. He did not stay at home. In Mark's gospel we find Jesus being busy on the Sabbath. Jesus taught in the synagogue on the Sabbath (Mark 1:21). He cast out demons on the Sabbath (Mark 1:23-25). He picked grain on the Sabbath (Mark 2:23). He also healed the sick on the Sabbath (Mark 3:1-5). Jesus was known for doing things differently and He would give a hint as to why. "And He was saying to them, "The Sabbath was made for man, not man, for the Sabbath. Consequently, the Son of Man is Lord even of the Sabbath" (Mark 2:27, 28).

Having now given some thought to all of this, what would it have been like that Sabbath, on the sixteenth of Nisan? Everyone knew

AN ACCOUNT OF EVENTS AFTER CHRIST'S CRUCIFIXION

Jesus would not be there at synagogue, but would they? Would they stay home out of fear or would they go out to hear what everyone now said and taught? Some would be sad and in mourning, while others would be elated about finally being rid of Jesus. Either way they would surely be divided about what had happened. Those who loved Him were still unsure, and those who rejected Him now had blood on their hands.

Nisan 17, - three days after Passover, the first day of the Jewish week.

It is the <u>third day</u> of the Feast of Unleavened Bread, which was three days after Passover, two days after the High Sabbath, and one day after the weekly Sabbath (John 19:31 and Matthew 26:1). This is the first day of the Jewish week and it started at 6 p.m. in the evening. To the Romans this would still be their seventh day, or Saturday, at 6 p.m. in the evening.

Nisan 17, The Resurrection – After the Sabbaths

"After the 'Sabbaths'... (Matthew 28:1), the Sabbath is plural here in the Greek text. The actual Greek text reads as follows: "After the <u>Sabbaths</u>, upon the dawning into the first to the <u>Sabbaths</u>, came Mary of Magdala and the other Mary came to see the tomb" (Matthew 28:1).

An in-depth look into Matthew 28:1, does not say what many translations have decided to put down for text. This action shows the common mistake of writing not the simple translation of the text, but the interpretation of the text. It is the mistake of trying to make it easier to be read, and in turn the reader does not know to search the Scriptures for themselves, as they should.

First, this verse confirms by saying "after the Sabbaths" (plural) that there were two Sabbaths. It was just prior to the morning of the first day of the week in the year of Jesus Christ's crucifixion. This verse, along with John 19:31, says that the day after He was crucified, was a 'High Sabbath,' and that day would then be followed by the regular weekly Sabbath. Second, the two consecutive Sabbaths are possible in Luke 23:53-56, where Joseph of Arimathea takes Jesus' body and lays it in a tomb (v 53). That day was the Preparation Day, or Passover, and the Sabbath drew near (which was the Feast of Unleavened Bread (v 54). The women followed and observed the tomb and how the body was laid. Then they returned to where they were staying and prepared the spices and fragrant oils (v 55). They then <u>rested</u> on the Sabbath (σάββατον), (singular, which would be the regular weekly Sabbath on the seventh day), according to the <u>commandment</u> (v 56).

Nisan 17, The Resurrection - The First Day of the Week

Now, continuing with the Greek translation and following what was just said, Luke 24:1 continues, "On the first day of the 'week'..." The word *week* is really Sabbaths (σαββάτων), plural in the Greek, just as recorded in Matthew 28:1. In fact, in all four gospels it is recorded the same way concerning *Sabbaths* and the word *week*. "After the Sabbaths (plural), at the dawning into the first *day* of the *week*, (Sabbaths) ..." (Matthew 28:1). Also, the word *day* 'is only implied, the actual word *day* 'is not there in the Greek.

"Very early in the morning, on the first *day* of the 'week,' (<u>Sabbaths</u>) ..." (Mark 16:2).

"On the first *day* of the 'week', (<u>Sabbaths</u>) ..." (Luke 24:1).

"On the first *day* of the 'week', (<u>Sabbaths</u>) ..." (John 20:1).

The question is, why do most translations, if not all Bible translations, use *week* instead of *Sabbaths*? This is because of the Jewish understanding of days of the week. It was said in Chapter One that the Jews did not name the days of the week other than the Sabbath. They used the Genesis account of the first day, the second day, etc. and the seventh day was the Sabbath rest. Therefore, as was said, the first *day* of the 'week,' or 'to the Sabbaths,' is the day as it relates to the Sabbaths. Whether referring to one week or any week, it is the 'day' as it relates to the Sabbaths. The first *day* to the Sabbaths would be their first *day* of the week. The regular Sabbaths would all be the end of the week. It is then okay to let the different Bible Versions and the interpretations stand, but it is not the proper translation of the actual wording. The use of the word *day* here is implied, and the use of *week* must be understood!

To recap this issue, the Jewish calendar does not have names for the days of the week. The seventh day of the week which is the word 'Sabbath' (Shabbat) is the exception. The days of the week are simply known as first day, second day, third day, etc. Sometimes the 'days' are referred to more fully as the First Day of the Sabbaths, etc. In Hebrew, the word 'Yom' equals Day.[3] Yom Rishon = First Day (Sun.), Yom Sheini = Second Day (Mon.), Yom Shlishi = Third Day (Tues.), Yom R'vi'I = Fourth Day (Weds.), Yom Chamishi = Fifth Day (Thur.), Yom Shishi = Sixth Day (Fri.) and Shabbat kodesh = holy Sabbath (Sat.)

Moving on, it needs to be shown that Jesus rose before the daylight hours of the seventeenth, the first day of the week. The scriptures say:

> "...while it was still dark..." (John 20:1) – the best of these Scriptures.
> "On the first day of the week, at early dawn..." (Luke 24:1) – probably while still dark, or just thereafter.
> "...when the sun had risen..." (Mark 16:2) – addressing as to when they got there.
> "...as it began to dawn toward the first day of the week..." (Matthew 28:1) – implying it was dark, becoming partially light.

As daylight approaches, and while it is dark, it is still the 'night' of the Nisan 17, the first day of the week. Although there seems to be different accounts of when the women went to the tomb, they are all saying the same thing. That is this; <u>Jesus was already risen from the dead</u> when they got there. This means while it was still dark on the first day of the week (the evening before the day).

Here is how that happened: "...toward <u>the first day of the week</u>, Mary Magdalene and the other Mary came to look at the grave. And behold, a severe earthquake had occurred, for an angel of the Lord descended from heaven and came and rolled away the stone and sat upon it. And his appearance was like lightning, and his clothing as white as snow. The guards shook for fear of him and became like dead men. The angel said... "He is not here, for He is risen." (Matthew 28:14, 6). "Now <u>after</u> He had risen early on the first day of the week, He first appeared to Mary Magdalene..." (Mark 16:9).

It is interesting to note that <u>all four</u> gospels say, "the first day of the week." This means it WAS the first day of the week to the Jews and, as will be shown, the first day of the week (Sunday) to the Romans too. This is because the Gospel of John uses Roman time. Therefore, with this understanding, it could have only been a Thursday Passover. Because, if not, Jesus would not of rose early in the morning on the first day of the week. All four gospels record a first day of the week resurrection because it was a Thursday Passover.

<u>Fact #4. Here Jesus rose from the dead on the first day of the week. This demonstrates the answer of the fourth fact in Chapter One that states this very thing.</u>

Nisan 17, The Resurrection – First Fruits

It is now the third day of the Feast of Unleavened Bread and the first day of the week. With His resurrection Jesus became the first fruits[4] of them that sleep. "He is the beginning, the first born from the dead" (Colossians 1:18). The scriptures say, "But now Christ has been raised from the dead, the first fruits of those who are asleep... in Christ all shall be made alive, but each in his own order. Christ the first fruits, after that those who are Christ's at His coming" (1 Corinthians 15:20-23).

With hindsight, the Jews should have known that another designated event would follow on their yearly days of appointed times. The fiftieth day that follows the weekly Sabbath after the Passover was a special day to them. Moses makes mention of this day as recorded in the Book of Leviticus.

> Then the Lord spoke to Moses, saying, "Speak to the sons of Israel and say to them, 'When you enter the land which I am going to give to you and reap its harvest, then you shall bring in the sheaf of the first fruits of your harvest to the priest. He shall wave the sheaf before the Lord for you to be accepted on the day after the Sabbath the priest shall wave it. Now on the day when you wave the sheaf, you shall offer a male lamb one year old without defect for a burnt offering to the Lord. Its grain offering shall then be two-tenths of an ephah of fine flour mixed with oil, an offering by fire to the Lord for a soothing aroma, with its drink offering, a fourth of a hin of wine. Until this same day, until you have brought in the offering of your God, you shall eat neither bread nor roasted grain nor new growth. It is to be a perpetual statute throughout your generations in all your dwelling places (Leviticus 23:9-14).

Can it be known that the Scriptures above apply to the day after this particular Sabbath? It is the Sabbath that followed the day when a male lamb of the first year without blemish was offered up (Passover Lamb)! Yes, it can because the Scriptures of Leviticus continues on to say: "You shall count for yourselves from the day after the Sabbath, from the day that you brought the sheaf of the wave offering; there shall be seven complete Sabbaths. You shall count fifty days to the day after the seventh Sabbath; then you shall present a new grain offering to the Lord" (Leviticus 23:15, 16).

The day after the Sabbath when the people brought the sheaf offering is fifty days prior to the Feast of Weeks. For it is also written: "Also, on the day of the first fruits, when you present a new grain offering to the Lord in your Feast of Weeks, you shall have a holy convocation. You shall do no laborious work" (Numbers 28:26). Seven Sabbaths would be the Feast of Weeks. It is fifty days later and is called the Feast of Pentecost,[5] which in the Greek, 'peninta,' equals fifty. Acts 2, verse 1 says, "When the Day of Pentecost had come..." Therefore, counting backward fifty days would be the day after the regular Sabbath following Passover. So, yes, this particular first day of the week, Jesus' resurrection, was the day that would lead to the fulfillment of the day of first fruits.

Jesus died on Passover, then He was raised after the second Sabbath. It was the first day of the week, fifty days before the Feast of Weeks (Pentecost). The first fruits are represented of the believers who would receive the first fruits of His Spirit at Pentecost. Because He lives, we shall live also. The Feast of Weeks, or Pentecost, and the first day (day of First Fruits) is fifty days after what event, or day, that everyone needs to mark it on their calendar? – **The Resurrection.**

"But if the Spirit of Him who raised Jesus from the dead dwells in you, He who raised Christ Jesus from the dead will also give life to your mortal bodies through His Spirit who dwells in you. And not only this, but also, we ourselves, having the <u>first fruits of the Spirit,</u> even we ourselves groan within ourselves, waiting eagerly for our adoption as sons, the redemption of our bodies" (Romans 8:11, 23).

Nisan 17, The Resurrection – The Third Day

The Scriptures record that Jesus said He would rise "on the third day" (Matthew 16:21). The previous sections showed us how that was fulfilled. Having already seen how the first day of the Feast of Unleavened Bread would be the first day, the regular Sabbath was then the second day and the first day of the week was the third day.

To help further with the explanation of the third day is something that the Apostle Paul said. He wrote, "For I delivered to you as of first importance what I also received, that Christ died for our sins according to the Scriptures, and that he was buried, and that He was raised on the third day according to the Scriptures" (1 Corinthians 15:3, 4). What Scriptures would that be? The minor prophet Hosea prophesied saying, "Come let us return to the Lord; for He has torn, but He will heal us; He has wounded us, but He will bandage us. He will revive us after two days; He will raise us up on the third day, that we may live before Him" (Hosea 6:1, 2). When Jesus died on the cross and gave up His Spirit, the Bible says, "And behold, the veil of the temple was torn in two from top to bottom; and the earth shook, and the rocks were split. The tombs were opened, and many bodies of the saints who had fallen asleep were raised; and coming out of the tombs after His resurrection, they entered the holy city and appeared to many" (Matthew 27;51-53). These saints, who are the *us* of Hosea's prophecy above, are those to whom Jesus had descended and preached to. They are the ones to whom it was said, "on the third day He will raise us up." They were the ones He did raise up the third day, but it was after Jesus' resurrection.

It is also believed that the sayings as to when Jesus would rise are referring to more than just one particular day, but also to a 'time period.' Jesus may have also been saying that He will be resurrected after a time period in which a body is surely dead beyond any doubt. That being after a period of three days! Three to five days after death – the body starts to bloat; the human body can double in size.

In addition, insect activity can be present. The microorganisms and bacteria produce extremely unpleasant odors called putrefaction.[6] These odors often alert others that a person is dead.

This may well be the reason Jesus waited until the fourth day before He raised Lazarus. No one could then deny his death was real, and that Jesus had the power to raise the dead. "Jesus said, "Remove the stone." Martha, the sister of the deceased, said to Him, "Lord, by now there is a stench, for he has been dead four days" (John 11:39). This also may be why the chief priests and pharisees told Pilate to set guards at the tomb until the third day, even though they quoted Jesus saying He would rise after three days in Matthew 27:62-66. Could it be they too knew the meaning behind the saying 'the third day.' This would insinuate that they did not care when Jesus said He would rise. What mattered to them was that He would be dead for three days, for after that He would be dead indeed.

Note that it was on the first day of the week when two disciples on the road to Emmaus said, "But we were hoping that it was He who was going to redeem Israel. Indeed, besides all this, today is the third day since these things happened" (Luke 24:21). Jesus rose from the dead anywhere **between** the late evening hours of Nisan 17 and the dawn of day. It must be remembered that the Jewish day began at 6 p.m. in the evening.

"Today (Nisan 17) is the third day." When they said this, Jesus had already risen before dawn. This shows they did not really understand what Jesus had told them. "For as yet they did not understand the Scripture, that He must rise again from the dead" (John 20:9). All they knew was that today was the third day since He died, and so that is it- He is dead indeed. Even though they had hoped that it was He who was going to redeem Israel. But all they really knew was the understanding of the rule of the third day.

This saying had nothing to do with the sign of Jonah or with when He would rise, they were never sure of that. They never said anything about Him rising from the dead, only that it had been this long since it all happened. In fact, they were astonished to hear that the women said He had risen (Luke 24:22). Jesus had said His disciples, were foolish and slow of heart to believe (Luke 24:25).

What follows now is the Apostle John's account according to Roman time, it is Sunday night now- at evening. "Now when it was evening on that day, the first *day* of the week, and when the doors were shut where the disciples were *together*, due to fear of the Jews, Jesus came and stood in the midst, and said to them, "Peace be with you" (John 20:19).

Jesus rose victoriously on the first day of the week, after being dead for three days and three nights. He is alive, and He rose on the third day as promised.

If Jesus would have said that He would rise from the dead 'today,' or on the 'same day,' He would of rose on the fifth day of the Jewish week. But He did not!

If Jesus would have said that He would rise from the dead in 'one day,' He would of rose on the sixth day of the Jewish week. But He did not!

If Jesus would have said that He would rise from the dead on the 'second day,' He would of rose on the seventh day of the Jewish week. But He did not!

If Jesus would have said that He would rise from the dead 'on the third day,' He would of rose on the first day of the Jewish week. He did say this, and He did rise on the third day. The sixth day of the week (Nisan 15) was the one day, the seventh day of the week (Nisan 16) was the two days, and the first day of the week (Nisan 17) was the three days, or the third day.

If Jesus said He would rise 'in three days,' He would of rose on the first day of the week. He did say this, and He rose in three days. The sixth day (Nisan 15) was in one day, the seventh day (Nisan 16) was in two days and the first day (Nisan 17) was in three days. Jesus rose on the first day of the week (Nisan 17).

If Jesus would have said that He would rise from the dead 'after three days,' He would have risen on the first day of the week (Nisan 17). And He did! The sixth day (Nisan 15) was after one day (the fifth weekday), the seventh day (Nisan 16) was after two days (the sixth weekday) and the first day (Nisan 17) was after the third day (the seventh weekday). "Now after <u>He had risen early on the first of the week</u>, He appeared first to Mary Magdalene..." (Mark 16:9).

<u>Fact #5. Here Jesus fulfills His own words and that of the prophets by rising from the dead after three days, which was the first day of the week. This shows the answers of the fifth fact in Chapter One that states this very thing.</u>

Our Savior and High Priest has come forth alive from the dead. The Resurrection is proof that Jesus' sacrifice was sufficient and acceptable as the Lord's Passover Lamb. As said, IT IS FINISHED. The Scriptures say, Cephas saw Jesus, then so did the eleven. After that over 500 brethren saw Him at once... after that James saw Him, then all the apostles. Then at last the Apostle Paul saw Him too (1 Corinthians 15:5-8).

> *"Blessed be the God and Father of our Lord Jesus Christ, who according to His great mercy has caused us to be born again to a living hope through the resurrection of Jesus Christ from the dead" (1 Peter 1:3).*

Consider this also about The Third Day.

- It was the third day after Jesus was crucified and buried that He came out of the tomb victorious over death and the grave.

- It was the third day after Passover when it was declared that He is not here, He is risen.
- It was the third day of the Feast of Unleavened Bread when Jesus rose from the dead.
- It was the third day of everything so that it could not be denied or missed somehow that He is risen indeed.

"For as yet they did not understand the Scripture, that He must rise again from the dead" (John 20:9).

Next! How did Jesus fulfill the requirements for the Passover Lamb whereby He ended up laying down His life as the Lamb of God?

CHAPTER SIX

THE REQUIREMENTS OF
THE PASSOVER LAMB

"Abraham said, "God will provide for
Himself the lamb for the burnt offering,
my son..." (Genesis 22:8).

JESUS FULFILLS ALL THAT THE LAW OF THE LORD REQUIRED
CONCERNING THE PASSOVER LAMB.

The Passover Lamb – Was Dying <u>on</u> Passover Enough?

Chapter One showed how the pre-set date of Passover, Nisan 14, was determined for each New Year. Then the rest of the feast days of the year were determined by knowing that date. Chapters Two through Five showed the biblical accounts of the week of Passover, the accounts of the Day of Passover itself, and then the three days that followed. In these four chapters it was shown how the Passover, on which Jesus died as the Passover Lamb, fell on the fifth day of the Jewish week. This finding is contrary to the traditionally accepted day of the crucifixion, which is the sixth day of the Jewish week, our Friday. Chapter Seven will again show how it truly was a Thursday Passover <u>and</u> the year that it most likely occurred.

The question asked in this chapter is this, 'Was Jesus dying on Passover enough to make Him the Passover Lamb of God,' as John the Baptist said? It will be shown how Jesus clearly fulfilled all that was required of Him to be the Passover Lamb. This would put an end to any future need for Passover feasts, celebrations, or sacrifices. The New Testament never again mentions any need for its observance or its necessity, for it is fulfilled.

In fact, to the contrary, as Paul writes the Galatians, "But now that you have known God, or rather to be known by God, how is it that you turn again to the weak and worthless elemental things, to which you desire again to be enslaved all over again? You observe days and months and seasons and years. I fear for you, lest I have labored over you in vain" (Galatians 4:9-11). It is the Christians who should know this better than most. Those of all faiths and nationalities who are being saved are not to hold to the Old Testament ritual requirements and add Jesus the Messiah to it. They should knowingly and willingly lay it all aside, for they too are now Christians. "Knowing that you were not redeemed with perishable things like silver or gold from your futile way of life inherited from your forefathers" (1 Peter 1:18).

The Passover Lamb – A Progressive Revelation:

It all begins by realizing that Jesus, as the Passover Lamb, is a progressive revelation from the Book of Genesis all the way to the Book of Revelation. Here are Scriptures that show just that.

1. "The Lord God made garments of skin for Adam and his wife and clothed them" (Genesis 3:21).

    It does not say here what the animal was, only that the Lord God Himself provided a covering for their sin by the shedding of an animal's blood; for that is how the skins were obtained.

2. "Again, she gave birth to his brother Abel. And Abel was a keeper of flocks, but Cain was a tiller of the ground. So, it came

about in the course of time that Cain brought an offering to the Lord of the fruit of the ground. Abel, on his part also brought of the firstlings of his flock and of their fat portions. And the Lord had regard for Abel and for his offering; but for Cain and for his offering He had no regard. Cain became very angry and his countenance fell" (Genesis 4:2-5).

Here it says the sacrificial offering was the <u>firstborn lamb</u> (Abel a keeper of sheep) which was acceptable to the Lord.

3. "Take now your son, <u>your only son, whom you love</u>, Isaac, and go to the land of Moriah, and offer him there as a burnt offering on one of the mountains of which I will tell you" (Genesis 22:2).

"But Isaac spoke to Abraham his father... 'Behold, the fire and the wood, but where is the lamb for the burnt offering? Abraham said, '<u>God will provide for Himself the lamb</u> for the burnt offering, my son..." (Genesis 22:7, 8).

Here it is saying that God would provide Himself (as) <u>the lamb</u> that would be sacrificed upon the wood and on that mountain. That mountain was later determined to be Mount Calvary. "For God <u>so loved</u> the world that He gave His <u>only begotten Son</u>..." (John 3:16), as the sin offering.

4. "Your lamb shall be an unblemished male a year old... The fourteenth day of the same month then the whole assembly of the congregation of Israel is to kill it at twilight. Moreover, they shall take some of the blood and put it on the two doorposts and on the lintel... It is the Lord's Passover" (Exodus 12:5-11).

The Lord's Passover lamb shall be a male without blemish. Jesus was the firstborn male and certainly without blemish ("...Him who knew no sin..." 2 Corinthians 5:21). Jesus too would be killed on Nisan 14 at twilight as all the people shouted, "...His blood be upon us and our children" (Matthew 27:25)! They too caused His blood to end up upon two pieces of wood that could likewise be doorposts. "Let it be known to all of you and to all the people of Israel, that by the name of Jesus Christ the Nazarene, <u>whom you crucified</u>..." (Acts 4:10). The people of Israel killed the Passover Lamb, along with the Roman soldiers and all of us who have sinned (Romans 3:23).

5. "Therefore, the Lord <u>Himself</u> will give you a sign: Behold, the virgin will be with child and bear a Son, and she will call His name Immanuel" (Isaiah 7:14). "For a child will be born to us, a Son will be given to us... And His name will be called... Mighty God, Eternal Father, Prince of Peace" (Isaiah 9:6).

This again speaks of Jesus. "For God so loved the world that He gave His only begotten Son..." (John 3:16). Jesus said... "He who has seen Me has seen the Father..." (John 14:9). "I and the Father are one" (John 10:30).

It was said, concerning Adam and Eve, that the Lord God Himself provided a covering for their sin. Also, concerning Abraham and Isaac, it was said, "God will provide HIMSELF the lamb."

Concerning the sign Isaiah said, "the Lord <u>Himself</u> will give you a sign." <u>The sign</u> is the Lord Himself, He is the Son given, He is Immanuel, He is Mighty God, Everlasting Father and Prince of Peace. Just as when Jesus comes again, He, Himself, will be the sign: "Then the sign of the Son of Man will appear in the sky... and they will see <u>the Son of Man</u> coming on the clouds of the sky with power and great glory" (Matthew 24:30).

God has supplied <u>Himself</u>, in the person of Jesus Christ, as the Passover Lamb slain for the sins of the world. He is also revealed as such in John's Revelation as the progression is continued. In the Book of Revelation, it says:

6. "And I saw between the throne (with the four living creatures) and the elders a Lamb standing, as if slain..." (Revelation 5:6). "And bow before it shall all who are dwelling upon the

land, whose names have not been written in the scroll of the life of the Lamb slain from the foundation of the world" (Revelation 13:8, Youngs Literal Translation-YLT).

From Genesis to Revelation – the Lamb slain for our sin.

Jesus Christ – Immanuel – God with us, having come in the flesh. The Lamb of God who takes away the sin of the world. Such Love, Such Wondrous Love!

The Passover Lamb – Jesus Fulfills the Law Requirements:

The following are eleven of the most defining Scripture references giving the requirements of the lamb for Passover. See how Jesus fulfills each reference, plus other shadows and types, and truly is our Passover Lamb.

#1. "Now the Lord said to Moses and Aaron in the land of Egypt, "This month shall be your beginning of months for you; it is to be the first month of the year to you. Speak to all the congregation of Israel, saying: On the tenth of this month, they are each one to take a lamb for themselves..." (Exodus 12:1-3). "Go and take (pick out) for yourselves lambs according to your families and slay the Passover lamb" (Exodus 12:21).

Jesus fulfills this. On the tenth of Nisan (Abib), Jesus is picked out as the people's choice when He rides into the city of Jerusalem fulfilling the prophecy of Zechariah 9:9. Chapter Three showed how this occurred on the tenth of the month as mentioned in Exodus Chapter Twelve.

"Say to the daughter of Zion, behold, your King is coming to you, gentle and mounted on a donkey... and those who followed, were shouting, "Hosanna to the Son of David! Blessed is He who comes in the name of the Lord" (Matthew 21:5-9 and Luke 19:38)!

#2. "Your lamb <u>shall be an unblemished male</u> a year old..." (Exodus 12:5).

Jesus fulfills this. Jesus was a male, the firstborn son, and certainly without blemish for He was without sin. "And Joseph... took Mary as his wife but kept her a virgin until she gave birth to a Son, and he call His name Jesus" (Matthew 1:25). "For He (God the Father) made Him (Jesus) who <u>knew no sin</u> to be sin on our behalf, so that we might become the righteousness of God in Him" (2 Corinthians 5:21).

"Then Pilate said to the chief priests and the crowd, <u>I find no guilt in this Man</u>" (Luke 23:4). "Pilate summoned the chief priests and the rulers and the people, and said to them, "You brought this man to me as one who incites the people to rebellion, and behold, having examined Him before you, I have found no guilt in this man regarding the charges which you make against Him. No, nor has Herod, for he sent Him back to us; and behold, nothing deserving death has been done by Him" (Luke 23:13-15).

The saying, 'without blemish' is a reference to being 'innocent,' 'blameless' and 'sinless.' Jesus, and only Jesus, was without blemish and sinless.

"For we do not have a high priest who cannot sympathize with our weaknesses, but One who has been tempted in all things as we are, yet without sin" (Hebrews 4:15). And finally, "Knowing that you were not redeemed with perishable things like silver or gold from your futile way of life inherited from your forefathers, but with precious blood, as of a lamb unblemished and spotless, the blood of Christ" (1 Peter 1:18, 19).

#3. "You are not allowed to sacrifice the Passover in any of your towns which the Lord your God is giving you; but at the place where the Lord your God chooses to establish His name, you shall sacrifice the Passover in the evening at sunset, at the time that you came out of Egypt" (Deuteronomy 16:5, 6). "...The Lord said to David and to Solomon his son, "In this house and in Jerusalem, which I have chosen from all the tribes of Israel, I will put My name forever" (2 Kings 21:7).

Jesus fulfills this. The Passover was to be celebrated only at Jerusalem and no other place. They then took Jesus from the city of Jerusalem to a place outside the city gates to suffer and die. That place was Golgotha, also called 'Calvary', from the Latin (Matthew 27:33).

> But Jesus, turning to them said, "Daughters of Jerusalem, stop weeping for Me, but weep for yourselves and for your children" (Luke 23:28). "They took Jesus, therefore, and He went out, bearing His own cross, to the place called the Place of a Skull, which is called in Hebrew, Golgotha. There they crucified Him, and with Him two other men, one on either side, and Jesus in between. Pilate also wrote an inscription and put it on the cross. It was written, "JESUS THE NAZARENE, THE KING OF THE JEWS." Therefore, many of the Jews read this inscription, for the place where Jesus was crucified was near the city; and it was written in Hebrew, Latin and in Greek (John 19:17, 20).

"For the bodies of those animals, whose blood is brought into the holy place by the high priest as an offering for sin, are burned outside the camp. Therefore, Jesus also, that He might sanctify the people through His own blood, suffered outside the gate" (Hebrews 13:11, 12). "And at the ninth hour Jesus cried out with a loud voice, 'Eloi, Eloi, lama sabachthani?' which is translated, 'My God, My God, why have You forsaken Me?' "And Jesus cried out with a loud voice and breathed His last" (Mark 15:34, 37). He died at 3 p.m.

#4. "You shall keep it until <u>the fourteenth day of the same month</u>, then the whole assembly of the congregation of Israel is to <u>kill it at twilight</u>" (Exodus 12:6).

Jesus fulfills this. It was the fourteenth of Nisan and it was at twilight, 3 p.m. to be exact. (See Chapter Three) "Now it was the day of preparation for the Passover (Nisan 14), it was about the sixth hour (6 a.m. Roman time). And he (Pilate) said to the Jews, Behold your King! So, they cried out, Away with Him, away with Him, crucify Him! ..." (John 19:14, 15).

> The Jews answered him, we have a law, and by that law He ought to die, because He made Himself out to be the Son of God" (John 19:7). "And <u>all the people</u> (the whole congregation) said, "His blood shall be on us and on our children" (Matthew 27:25). "Now Caiaphas was the one who advised the Jews that it was expedient for one man to die on behalf of the people" (John 18:14 and John 11:50). "It was the third hour (9 a.m. Jewish time), and <u>they crucified Him</u>" (Mark 15:25). "It was now about the sixth hour, and darkness fell over the whole land until the ninth hour, because the sun was obscured; and the veil of the temple was torn in two. And Jesus, crying out with a loud voice, said, "Father, into Your hands I commit My spirit." Having said this, He breathed His last" (Luke 23:44-46). "...He said, "It is finished! And bowing His head, He gave up His spirit." (John 19, verse 30.)

#5. "Moreover, they shall <u>take some of the blood</u> and <u>put it on the two door posts</u> and on the lintel of the houses in which they eat it" (Exodus12:7).

Jesus fulfills this. The blood of His head, back and feet were upon the vertical wooden post and the blood of his hands, shoulders and back were upon the horizontal wooden post that formed the cross at Golgotha. "Now the men who were holding Jesus in custody were mocking Him and beating Him" (Luke 22:63). The men smote him. In the Greek, the word 'smote' means scourge. It was a form of punishment from the law that the Jews could use to deter wickedness; read about this in Deuteronomy 25:1-3. Of course, this action was abused by the hypocritical leadership, especially in Jesus' day. Paul was also a victim of this same injustice (2 Corinthians 11:24).

History records the Romans also using this method of torture and chastisement. A whip with nine cords on a handle that each had a small piece of bone or glass or some object that would tear small pieces of flesh out of one's body, as slapped across the back. It was called the cat-o'-nine-tails. The law allowed for forty stripes. Usually, the scourging process was 39 times, 40 minus one, to be sure not to go over 40 by mistake, thus breaking the law. The Roman government perfected this form of punishment that would inflict the most pain without killing the victim. Although the Scriptures do not directly say that Jesus was whipped in such a manner, they do say He was scourged.

"But He was pierced for our offenses, He was crushed for our wrong doings; the punishment for our well-being was laid upon Him, and by His wounds we are healed" (Isaiah 53:5 and 1 Peter 2:24). "Pilate then took Jesus and scourged Him" (John 19:1). "And after twisting together a crown of thorns, they put it on His head, and a reed in His right hand; and they knelt down before Him and mocked Him, saying, Hail King of the Jews! They spat on Him and took the reed and began to beat Him on the head" (Matthew 27:29, 30). Also, read Psalm 22:1-18.

"But Thomas... said to them, "Unless I see in His hands the imprint of the nails... I will not believe" (John 20:24, 25). Upon His resurrection, Jesus said to His disciples, "See My hands and My feet, that it is I Myself..." (Luke 24:39). "For this is My blood of the new covenant, which is shed for many for the remission of sins" (Matthew 26:28).

#6. "They shall <u>eat the flesh</u> that same night; roasted with fire, and… <u>with unleavened bread.</u>.." (Exodus 12:8).

Jesus fulfills this. Jesus used His body and blood repeatedly as that which needs partaken of, figuratively, in order to be redeemed. For He is the true manna that came down from heaven that can enable one to never hunger and thirst again and to live forever. Jesus' sinless life speaks of bread without leaven. He was born in the City of Bread, Bethlehem (Matthew 2:1), and He is called 'The Bread of Life' (John 6:35).

"So, Jesus said to them, "Truly, truly, I say to you, unless you eat the flesh of the Son of Man and drink His blood, you have no life in yourselves. He who eats My flesh and drinks My blood has eternal life, and I will raise him up at the last day. For My flesh is true food, and My blood is true drink. This is the bread which came down out of heaven; not as your fathers ate and died; he who eats this bread will live forever" (John 6:53-55, 58). "I am the bread of life" (John 6:48).

#7. "For I will go through the land of Egypt on that night and will strike down all the firstborn in the land of Egypt, both man and beast; and against all the gods of Egypt <u>I will execute judgment</u>: I am the Lord" (Exodus 12:12).

Jesus fulfills this. Our Lord and Savior will execute judgment upon all the gods and godless of this world, of which Egypt is a type.

"For not even the Father judges anyone but has given all judgment to the Son" (John 5:22). "And He gave Him authority to execute judgment, because He is the Son of Man" (John 5:27). "I can of nothing on My own initiative (of Myself). As I hear, I judge; and My judgment is just, because I do not seek My own will, but the will of the Him who sent Me" (John 5:30). (Hearing a voice from heaven) "Jesus answered and said, this voice has not come for My sake, but for your sakes. Now judgment is upon this world; now the ruler of this world will be cast out. And I, if I am lifted up from the earth, will draw all men to Myself" (John 12:30-32).

#8. "The blood shall be a sign for you on the houses where you live; and when I see the blood, I will pass over you..." (Exodus 12:13).

Jesus fulfills this. When the Father looks at us, He does not see our sin but the blood of Christ which cleanses us from all sin (1 John 1:7b). The judgment of God, placed upon Christ while on that cross, has passed over us.

> And according to the Law, one may almost say, all things are cleansed with blood, and without shedding of blood there is no forgiveness (of sin). ...He has been manifested to put away sin by the sacrifice of Himself. And since it is appointed for men to die once and after this comes the judgment, so Christ having been offered once to bear the sins of many... (Hebrews 9:22, 26-28). Christ has redeemed us from the curse of the law, having become a curse for us, for it is written, "Cursed is everyone who hangs on a tree" (Galatians 3:13 and Deuteronomy 21:23). He has canceled out the certificate of debt consisting of decrees against us, which was hostile to us; and He has taken it out of the way, having nailed it to the cross (Colossians 2:14). We know that we were not redeemed with perishable things like silver and gold from your futile way of life inherited from your forefathers, but with the precious blood, as of a lamb unblemished and spotless, the blood of Christ (1 Peter 1:18, 19).

#9. "Now this day will be a memorial to you, and you shall celebrate it as a feast to the Lord; throughout your generations..." (Exodus 12:14).

Jesus fulfills this. Not a memorial of Passover but of Him, the Passover Lamb, and what He has done for you.

"And when He had given thanks, He broke it and said, "This is My body, which is for you; do this in remembrance of Me." In the same way He took the cup also after supper, saying, "This cup is the new covenant in My blood; do this, as often as you drink it, in remembrance of Me." For as often as you eat this bread and drink the cup, you proclaim the Lord's death until He comes" (1 Corinthians 11:24-26). A memorial unto Jesus.

#10. "It is to be eaten in a single house; you are not to bring forth any of the flesh outside of the house, <u>nor are you to break any bone of it</u>" (Exodus 12:46).

Jesus fulfills this. Only the King James Versions says, Take eat; this is My body which is _broken_ for you. But the original Greek text does not include the word _broken_, because it was not broken. The scriptures say:

"So, the soldiers came, and broke the legs of the first and of the other who was crucified with Him; but coming to Jesus, when they saw that he was already dead, <u>they did not break his legs</u>. But one of the soldiers pierced His side with a spear, and immediately blood and water came out. For these things came to pass to fulfill the Scripture, "Not a bone of His shall be broken." And again, another Scripture says, "They shall look on Him whom they pierced" (John 19:32-34 and 36-37, and Numbers 9:12; Zechariah 12:10).

1 Corinthians 11:24 should read, as from the original Greek, "This is My body which is for you." Yes, Jesus was beaten and bruised, but <u>not broken</u>, not a broken bone nor a broken spirit.

#11. "Then the Lord spoke to Moses, saying, <u>Sanctify to Me every firstborn,</u> the first offspring of every womb among the sons of Israel, both of man and beast; it belongs to Me." It came to about, when Pharaoh was stubborn about letting us go, that the Lord killed every firstborn in the land of Egypt, both the firstborn of man and the firstborn of beast. Therefore, I sacrifice to the Lord the males, the first offspring of every womb, but every <u>firstborn of my sons I redeem</u>" (Exodus 13:1, 2, 15).

Jesus fulfills this. This is the memorial of the Passover. The disobedient (Egyptians) lost their firstborn and the obedient, those who applied the blood of the Lamb, had the lives of their firstborn spared. Jesus was the firstborn of Joseph and Mary and so they did as Moses directed, commemorating the firstborns that were spared because the Lord passed over the houses of the children of Israel.

> And when eight days had passed, before His circumcision, His name was then called Jesus, the name given by the angel before He was conceived in the womb. And when the days for their purification according to the law of Moses were completed, they brought Him up to Jerusalem to present Him to the Lord (as it is written in the Law of the Lord, "Every firstborn male that opens the womb shall be called holy to the lord"), and to offer a sacrifice according to what was said in the Law of the Lord..." When they had performed all things according to the law of the Lord, they returned to Galilee, to their own city of Nazareth (Luke 2:21-24, 39).

The Passover Lamb – Jesus Fulfills Shadows and Types:

There are many Shadows and Types of Christ in the Old Testament; these are people or events that speak of Christ. An example would be the 'rock' that brought forth water in the wilderness (Numbers 20:8). Scripture says, "And all drank the same spiritual drink, for they were drinking from a spiritual rock which followed them; and that rock was Christ" (1 Corinthians 10:4). And again, "Therefore no one is to act as your judge in regard to food or drink or in respect to a festival or a new moon or a Sabbath day— things which are a mere shadow of what is to come, but the substance belongs to Christ" (Colossians 2:16, 17). Here the judging was not for 'doing' but for 'not doing.' The

Judaizers were judging them because they did not observe these things any longer. Also, "For the Law, since it has only a shadow of the good things to come and not the very form of things, can never, by the same sacrifices which they offer continually year by year, make perfect those who draw near" (Hebrews 10:1). "...who serve a copy and shadow of the heavenly things..." (Hebrews 8:5). So too it is true that there are shadows and types referring to the Passover Lamb and to the Crucifixion.

Jesus also fulfills these types and shadows of Himself as the Passover Lamb

1. The sacrifice for **Adam and Eve** was a shadow from Genesis 3:21. Jesus was the Lamb slain from the foundation of the world that would do more than merely cover the sin of mankind. Jesus' sacrifice would remove the sin of those whom He would redeem as far as the east is from the west (Psalm 103:12).

2. **Able** was a type from Genesis 4:2-5. Jesus too was the firstborn, and His sacrifice was acceptable to the Lord, how much more so the precious blood of Christ than the blood of bulls and goats. "For it is impossible for the blood of bulls and goats to take away sins" (Hebrews 10:4). He is both Sheep, as Abel's sacrifice was, and Shepherd (John 10:11).

3. **Isaac** was a type from Genesis 22:7, 8. Jesus is the only begotten Son of the Father, the one whom the Father loved. He too willingly carried the wood up the hill to offer up Himself as a living sacrifice in complete obedience to the Father, with the promise of the Father that He would return again (John 10:17, 18).

4. **Joseph** was a type from Genesis 37:20-24 and Genesis 40:40. Jesus too was rejected by His brethren and left for dead. But He also rose up to sit at the right hand of all power

and had authority to rule over His brethren (Colossians 3:1), who left Him for dead.

5. **Moses** was a type from Numbers 21:8, 9. Moses lifted up the brass serpent on the pole in order that they who looked upon it would then have the plagued stayed in their behalf. Likewise, Jesus said about lifting up the serpent in the wilderness, "even so must the Son of Man be lifted up" (John 3:14). Now we, who are plagued by sin, need only look to Him and we will be saved.

6. **Isaiah** spoke of a lamb as a shadow from Isaiah 53:7. Jesus opened not His mouth and as He was being led as a lamb to the slaughter, and as a sheep before its shearers in silence (Isaiah 53:7). The crowd said, "He saved others let Him save Himself" (Luke 23:35). If this was to be true and He was to save others, He needed to keep silent. "And while being reviled, He did not revile in return; while suffering, He uttered no threats, but kept entrusting Himself to Him who judges righteously" (1 Peter 2:23). Although He could have called 10,000 angels, He just said, "Father forgive them, they know not what they do" (Luke 23:34).

The Passover Lamb – JESUS

Jesus fulfills Passover because Passover, like the Rock in the wilderness, the serpent on the pole, the priests, the sacrifices, the temple, the lamb and nearly everything, is a shadow or type of Him, and fulfilled by His life, death and resurrection.

He is the sacrifice for sin- there is now no other; He is the Passover Lamb- there is no other to be looking for, bought, sold, sacrificed, or celebrated. He is our Great High Priest that ever lives and sits at the right hand of the Father making intercession for us- there is no need for other priests who themselves have sin and die.

Not only did Jesus fulfill the Feast of Passover but the Feast of

Unleavened Bread; for He is the Bread of Life without sin, which the leaven represents symbolically. These were all earthy examples to be fulfilled when the spiritual reality had come. Jesus fulfilled the day of First Fruits, being the first fruits of them that sleep, when He rose from the dead on the first day of the week; the day after the Sabbath following Passover (Leviticus 23:5-11 and 1 Corinthians 15:20-23). The celebration of this fulfillment is now on what we call our Easter.

Jesus fulfilled these first three major feasts named above at His first coming. He later would also fulfill the Feast of Weeks, the feast 49 days after Easter, on Pentecost, by sending the Holy Spirit to fill His disciples with power. The bread of this feast offering is baked <u>with</u> leaven because, even though the Holy Spirit would be poured out upon us, and be in us, we would still have sin in our lives (Leviticus 23:16, 17; Acts 1:8; Acts 2:1; Acts 16:21, 33; 1 John 1:8-10).

Fact #6. <u>Jesus fulfilled the requirements of the Passover Lamb and therefore fulfilled Passover also</u>. <u>This shows the answer of the sixth fact in Chapter One that states this very thing.</u>

"Behold, the Lamb of God who takes away the sin of the world" (John 1:29).

"For this is My blood of the new covenant, which is shed for many for the remission of sins" (Matthew 26:28).

*"Then I looked, and I heard the voice of many angels around the throne and the living creatures and the elders; and the number of them was myriads of myriads, and thousands of thousands, saying with a loud voice, **"Worthy is the Lamb that was slain** to receive power and riches and wisdom and might and honor and glory and blessing."* And every created thing which is in heaven and on the earth and under the earth and on the sea, and all things in them, I heard saying, "To Him who sits on the throne, and to the Lamb,*

be blessing and honor and glory and dominion forever and ever"
(Revelation 5:11-13).

Let us now take a close look into the Historical Account of that Passover and Crucifixion and verify the days and dates whereby Jesus ended up laying down His life as the Lamb of God.

CHAPTER SEVEN

HISTORICAL ACCOUNT OF THIS PASSOVER / CRUCIFIXION

"When He began His ministry, Jesus Himself was about thirty years of age, being as was supposed, the son of Joseph, the son of Eli..." (Luke 3:23).

The Ministry of John the Baptist

When did all of this take place in history? It happened when God intervened in Roman history and used it to fulfill Jewish history for His glory. Those who walked in darkness would see a great light (Isaiah 9:2). The Scriptures will tell when this occurred through the names and dates that are given.

"Now in the <u>fifteenth year</u> of the reign of Tiberius Caesar, when Pontius Pilate was governor of Judaea, and Herod was tetrarch of Galilee, and his brother Philip was tetrarch of the region Ituraea and of Trachonitis, and Lysanias was tetrarch of Abilene, in the high priesthood of Annas and Caiaphas, <u>the word of God came to John, the son of Zacharias,</u> in the wilderness. And he came into the district around the Jordon, preaching a baptism of repentance for the forgiveness of sins" (Luke 3:1-3). From these verses it can be deduced approximately when John the Baptist began his ministry and then try to figure when Jesus began His ministry. Tiberius

Caesar began his reign as Emperor in 14 A.D., therefore 14 A.D. plus fifteen years equals 29 A.D. History records that in 29 A.D. these individuals ruled:[1]

Pontius/ Pilate and Caiaphas ruled, (until 36 A.D.)
Herod Antipas ruled as tetrarch of Galilee, (until 39 A.D.)
Philip ruled as tetrarch of Ituraea, (until 34 A.D.)
Lysanias ruled as tetrarch of Abilene (in A.D. 28-29)
[Herod the Great died in 1 B.C.]

John was six months older than Jesus (Luke 1:24-27, 36-38) and Jesus was born before Herod died in 1 B.C. (Matthew 2:19). Therefore, they would both be over thirty years of age when they began their ministries no matter what the year was. John the Baptist began his ministry in the fifteenth year of the reign of Tiberius Caesar, which was in the year 29 A.D. John was probably at least thirty years old, because the Book of Numbers tells us repeatedly that those who are to enter into service, to do work in the tabernacle, must be at least thirty years old (Numbers 3:23, 30, 35, 39, 43, 47). This was like the minimum age requirement for 'the work of the Lord' at the time. For argument sake, let us say John is at least thirty years of age sometime in the year 29 A.D., and the word of the Lord comes to Him shortly after; anywhere from three to six months later. It could now be close to the winter of 29 A.D. or nearing the Spring of 30 A.D. at most.

With John being six months older than his cousin Jesus, Jesus too would be at least 30 years of age around this same time of year, late 29 A.D. or early 30 A.D. Although Jesus' ministry would not begin until three things occurred. First, of course, Jesus would fulfill the law of Numbers Chapter Three as mentioned before, and He would need to be at least thirty years of age. Scripture tells us: "When He began His ministry, Jesus Himself was about <u>thirty years of age</u>, being as was supposed, the son of Joseph, the son of Eli..."

(Luke 3:23). Jesus being thirty years of age, or there about, means He could be a month or two, or even a year or two, older. It is well into the year 30 A.D., and there are no scriptures saying exactly how long John's ministry lasted. It is not John's or Jesus' ages that are important here, but the year is very important.

Second, Jesus would have to give John a chance to fulfill His calling; the spreading the message of repentance and of the coming of the Anointed One. John would have to point Jesus out and identify Him as the lamb of God. During his ministry John would baptize Jesus to fulfill all righteousness (Matthew 3:15). John's ministry would come to an end with his imprisonment, and death. Third, and finally, Jesus would then have to face His own trials and temptations, in the power of the Spirit, through a wilderness experience, and come out victorious. "And He was in the wilderness forty days being tempted by Satan; and He was with the wild beasts, and the angels were ministering to Him" (Mark 1:13). He then went forth in the power of the Holy Spirit. Jesus is ready to now come on the scene and begin His Ministry as Messiah.

The Prophet Daniel

Although not necessary, the minor prophet Daniel may help to show the year of 30 A.D. as being the acceptable beginning of Jesus' ministry here on earth. In the opening verses of Daniel Chapter Nine it says: "In the first year of Darius, the son of Ahasuerus... I Daniel, observed in the books the numbers of the years which was revealed as the word of the Lord to Jeremiah the prophet, for the completion of the desolations of Jerusalem, namely, seventy years." (Daniel 9:1, 2).

The part of those scriptures that are of interest here are in verse twenty-five of Chapter Nine. "So you are to know and discern that from the issuing of a decree to restore and rebuild Jerusalem until Messiah the Prince there will be seven weeks and sixty-two weeks;

it will be built again, with plaza and moat, even in times of distress" (Daniel 9:25).

This verse says, *until Messiah,* insinuating when He comes on the scene or makes Himself known. This will be many years after a decree is issued to go and restore and rebuild Jerusalem. The total amount of time is at least seven weeks plus sixty-two weeks which equals sixty-nine weeks. Each week is a period of seven years, therefore sixty-nine times seven equals 483 years. The verse says between the decree and until Messiah will be seven weeks and sixty-two weeks. The reason for dividing it into seven weeks (the first forty-nine years) and sixty-two weeks (the last 434 years) is not given, but there must have been two segments to it. Otherwise, why not just say sixty-nine weeks instead of *seven weeks and sixty-two weeks?* This is believed to be the reason there are so many of views on interpreting this verse. No one considers a delay of time between the two periods of weeks, the same way a delay exists between the sixty-ninth and seventieth week. This fact alone makes it almost impossible to decide upon exact dates. Either way the total weeks after the decree would then be no less than sixty-nine weeks (or at least 483 years until Messiah).

Knowing when the decree was issued would have been extremely helpful, but since there have been several decrees with controversial dates, so that does not seem to be the way to go either. The first would have been the decree of Cyrus II.,[2] King of Persia in the year 538 B.C. to build the house of God (Ezra 1:1-4 and Ezra 5:13). Cyrus II was king from 539 to 529 B.C. It was 160 years before Cyrus was born that God choose him to make his decree (Isaiah 44:28 and Isaiah 45:1-4). King Artaxerxes and King Darius were both used by God to fulfill King Cyrus' original decree. The only sure thing here is the original decree would follow the year 539 B.C.

The other problem some seem to fall into with interpreting this verse is the issue of solar and lunar years, and Hebrew and Julian calendars. There seems to be a lot of gymnastics going on for nothing. The Metonic[3] cycle, in chronology, is a period of nineteen years in which there are 235 lunations, or synodic months, after which the Moon's phases recur on the same days of the solar year, or year of the seasons. The Jewish calendar[4] is based on the lunar year with an average of 12.36 (235 lunations divided by nineteen years) month per lunar year. The twelve months alternate between thirty and twenty-nine days per month. One more day is added for each leap year. This gives an average of 29.5 days per month. 12.36 months per lunar year times 29.5 average days per month equals 364.62 days per lunar year. The Julian calendar has 365 days a year, with one added day for each leap year. As one can see there is no need to go into lengthy figuring and equations to make a date in time fit the 483-year theories.

Without doing a commentary on the Book of Daniel, it is also possible to work backwards from what is known. Jesus began His ministry being about thirty years old (Luke 3:23). The year 30 A.D. was also confirmed from historical figures and given dates in the Bible (Luke 3:1-3). 434 years earlier, began the sixty-two weeks *until Messiah*. 30 A.D. minus 434 years goes back to the year 404 B.C. that the sixty-two weeks would have begun. What was going on at this time in history concerning the Jews and Jerusalem?

The most applicable thing in the year 404 B.C. is the end of the reign of King Darius of Persia (424 – 404 B.C.). The Persian kings had been very good to the Jews; King Cyrus, Artaxerxes, and Darius. The Peloponnesian wars had also just come to an end and Sparta became the most powerful city-state. The Greeks and the Egyptians would now be rivals in that area for power. The Greeks would prevail until the times of the Romans (Daniel 2:39, 40 and Daniel 8:21, 22). The city of Jerusalem would be in the crosshairs of competing powers.

This began the four hundred years of the Silence of Scripture. There was no word of the Lord in the land. The Levite records were only kept until the end of Darius' reign. "As for the Levites, the head of households were registered...so were the priests in the reign of Darius the Persian" (Nehemiah 12:22). The end of the book of Malachi, written prior to 400 B.C., begins the period of silence as the last book of the Old Testament. The book itself ends with a reference to the coming of John the Baptist (Malachi Chapter Three).

What about the *seven weeks* or forty-nine years that was to precede the *sixty-two weeks* (or 434 years)? This could be any time after the decree of 538 B.C. and up till 404 B.C. The hint may be in the verse when it says, "it will be built again, with plaza and moat, even in <u>times of distress</u>" (Daniel 9:25).

> "Then the people of the land discouraged the people of Judah, and frightened them from building, and bribed advisers against them to frustrate their advice all the days of Cyrus king of Persia, even until the reign of Darius king of Persia" (Ezra 4:4, 5). "Then work on the house of God in Jerusalem was discontinued, and it was stopped until the second year of the reign of Darius king of Persia" (Ezra 4:24).

If the work was stopped until the second year of the reign of King Darius that would be until 422 B.C., then the building in times of distress could be the forty-nine years or so preceding. Scripture says the work was frustrated *all the days of Cyrus king of Persia, even until the reign of Darius king of Persia.* The exact dates are insignificant, but probably between the years 475 B.C. and 425 B.C. Then the delay between the 'seven weeks' and the 'sixty-two weeks,' which begin in 404 B.C. 434 years later brings us to the year 30 A.D. and would satisfy the requirement of the years, or weeks, *until Messiah.* 30 A.D. is the year Jesus is revealed, not born, and when His ministry would begin.

The Ministry of Jesus Christ

Until Messiah the Prince, signifies Jesus is ready to begin His ministry. Jesus is at least thirty years old; He has been baptized (Matthew 3:13-17), the Holy Spirit has come upon Him (Luke 4:1), and He has withstood forty days and forty nights of the devil's temptations without sinning (Luke 4:13-15). To be slightly more than generous, say that another six months may have passed. It could be near or after the Fall of 30 A.D. According to Luke 2:41, Joseph and Mary went to the Passover celebration in Jerusalem every year as was according to the custom. Jesus did likewise as was custom, and there are at least three Passovers that can be identified.

- **(John 2, verse 13)**, "The Passover of the Jews was near, and Jesus went up to Jerusalem." (This is more than likely the Passover of 31 A.D.)

After John baptized Jesus, Jesus' ministry was now about choosing His disciples (John Chapter One). Jesus then performed His first miracle in His disciple's presence prior to this Passover of 31 A.D., for His ministry had begun (John Chapter Two). It was after this Passover that He was with His disciples in Judea, and they were baptizing, as John was (John 3:22).

John had not yet been imprisoned (John 3:24), for he was still giving witness to the Christ and saying that he was not the Christ (John 3:27-31). Jesus would not go to Galilee until John fulfilled his calling having been cast into prison. They were like a tag team; John had prepared the way, doing an excellent job in taking a stand for truth and righteousness and against sin, and now Jesus would take it from here. They both would end up giving their lives to fulfill their callings.

Therefore, when the Lord knew that the Pharisees had heard that Jesus was making and baptizing more disciples than John, (although Jesus Himself was not baptizing, but his disciples were), He left Judea, and went away again into Galilee (John 4:1-3). Now when He had heard that John had been taken into custody, He withdrew into Galilee; and leaving Nazareth, He came and settled in Capernaum... From that time Jesus began to preach and say, Repent, and believe in the gospel (Matthew 4:12, 13, 17).

It was after John was in prison and his ministry came to an end, that Jesus would take His ministry from Judea to Galilee. He would start by preaching the same message of repentance. It is was easily the middle of 30 A.D. in which Jesus started His ministry being about 30 years of age? This will be important as we move forward. At least a half a year had past, and it was now sometime <u>after</u> the Spring Passover of 31 A.D.

- **(John 5, verse 1)** "After these things there was a feast of the Jews, and Jesus went up to Jerusalem." (This may not have been a Passover feast, if so then 32 A.D.)
- **(John 6, verse 4)** "Now the Passover, the feast of the Jews, was near." (This is the Passover of 33 A.D.)
- **(John 11, verse 55)** "Now the Passover of the Jews was near, and many went up to Jerusalem out of the country before the Passover to purify themselves." (This is the beginning of the Passover of 34 A.D.)
- **(John 19, verse 31)** "Then the Jews, because it was the Day of Preparation (Passover), so that the bodies would not remain on the cross on the Sabbath (for that sabbath was a high day)..." (This is the end of the Passover of 34 A.D.)

The Passover of John Chapter Eleven is the same Passover of John Chapter Twenty. Chapter Eleven is the beginning of the week before Passover, and Chapter Twenty is the end. This Passover would also be Jesus' last. Some question whether Jesus did actually attend all four of the Passovers. They say this because the high priest prophesied that Jesus would die for the nation (John 11:51), or because from then on, they plotted to put Him to death (John 11:53)? Do you think He was afraid of that or of anything else? The answer to that is no, of course not. It is believed that He did attend them all, for Jesus was required by the law to attend Passover in Jerusalem (Deuteronomy 16:16). There is not one Passover that Jesus did not attend, but there may be one not recorded.

The belief is that Jesus' ministry lasted 3 ½ years:

The Fall of 30 A.D. to the Fall of 31 A.D. = 1 year
The Fall of 31 A.D. to the Fall of 32 A.D. = 2 years
The Fall of 32 A.D. to the Fall of 33 A.D. = 3 years
The Fall of 33 A.D. to the Spring of 34 A.D. = 3 ½ years

Parables Relating to Jesus' Ministry

This thinking is not just because of the number of Passovers recorded but because of Daniels vision of the seventy weeks (years) determined upon Jerusalem. Before that is looked at again, there are a couple of interesting parables in the gospel of Luke. The first is the parable found in Luke Chapter Thirteen:

And He began telling this parable: A man had a fig tree which had been planted in his vineyard; and he came looking for fruit on it and did not find any. And he said to the vineyard-keeper, "Behold, for three years I have come looking for fruit on this fig tree without finding any. Cut it down! Why does it even use up the ground?" And he answered and said to him, "Let it alone, sir, for this year too, until I dig around it and put in fertilizer; and if it bears fruit next year, fine; but if not, cut it down" (Luke 13:6-9).

The man is God Himself; the vineyard is the earth in general and Israel in particular. The fig tree He planted is Israel in general, (which symbolically is, at times, the fig tree[5]), and Jerusalem in particular. God came in human form as the Lord Jesus Christ and seeking fruit from Israel. At this point in time, it was after three years of ministry, and He found none. The keepers of the vineyard are the religious leaders, known as the vinedressers of the second parable in Luke Chapter 20, which shows that after the three years they still did not bear fruit.

The owner of the vineyard said, "What shall I do? I will send my beloved son; perhaps they will respect him." But when the vine-growers saw him, they reasoned with one another, saying, "This is the heir; let us kill him so that the inheritance will be ours." So, they threw him out of the vineyard and killed him. What, then, will the owner of the vineyard do to them? He will come and destroy these vine-growers and will give the vineyard to others. When they heard it, they said, "May it never be" (Luke 20:13-16)!

This parable, given later, now adds more detail and greater significance. God is the owner of the vineyard and the focus is more than Israel in particular- it is the world in general. "For God so loved the world that He gave His only begotten Son that whosoever believes in Him shall not perish but have everlasting life" (John 3:16).

The Jews rejected Jesus instead of giving the honor and glory that was due Him. "He came to His own, and those who were His own did not receive Him" (John 1:11). Here the vinedressers, or religious leaders, plotted among themselves how they would kill Him. After a mock trial and an appeal to Roman authority the Sinless Son of God was taken outside the city and crucified.

Now back to the prophet Daniel who went on to say: "Then after the sixty-two weeks (and seven weeks) the Messiah will be cut off and have nothing (but not for Himself, NKJV)..." (Daniel 9:26a). This happened when Jesus was cut-off, crucified as the Passover Lamb, after three and half years of ministry.

"...What then will the owner of the vineyard do to them? He will come and destroy those vine-growers and will give the vineyard to others..." (Luke 20:15, 16). Daniel goes on to say: "...And the people of the prince who is to come will destroy the city and the sanctuary. And its end will come with a flood; even to the end there will be war; desolations are determined" (Daniel 9:26b). That is what God did in 70 A.D. when He allowed the Romans (*the people* or soldiers *of the prince*- Titus- *who was to come*) to destroyed Jerusalem.[6] It was God's vengeance because of the blood of the prophets and the rejection of their Messiah in the day of His visitation. This was the completion of desolations (Daniel 9:2).

If assumed properly, Jesus' ministry began in the Fall of 30 A.D., then three and a half years of ministry would bring it to the Spring of 34 A.D., thus confirming all assumptions. All this Scriptural information is to confirm that Jesus' ministry truly lasted for three and a half years. His ministry followed that of John the Baptist's at the end of 29 A.D. and probably began in the Fall of 30 A.D. and ended in the Spring at the Passover of 34 A.D.

Let us now look into how an actual date for this Passover and the crucifixion of Jesus Christ can be established.

CHAPTER EIGHT

THE ESTABLISHING OF A ROMAN DATE

"This is the day which the Lord has made; Let us rejoice and be glad in it" (Psalm 118:24).

Establishing a Roman Date for Passover / Crucifixion:

Being very generous with the estimates of times and dates presented, the Crucifixion must have taken place at least between the years 32 and 36 A.D. This chapter will show how the days and dates obtained for Passover in the earlier chapters are confirmed from the information taken from the United States Naval Observatory Applications Department.[1] The Naval Applications Department has well documented the days and dates following the same requirements mentioned in Chapter One.

Looking at the information, the only year that meets the requirements is <u>34 A.D.</u> on the Julian Calendar. For this to be the correct year of the Passover, our Lord's crucifixion and His resurrection, it must also meet the requirements of the sign of the Prophet Jonah, which is to be three days and three nights in the heart of the earth. This would also mean that the resurrection would take place after the third night and before the fourth day, with Jesus rising on the first day of the week. A date that fits perfectly is one that has been determined by the United States Naval Observatory.

Chapters One through Four showed how the Jewish days and hours were determined. Knowing when the calendar year began, and then the date of Passover, makes it possible to create a Hebrew calendar for the first month and then for the rest of the year.

The following is a quick explanation of Figures 2 through 5 with information from the U.S. Naval Observatory's findings.

Figure 2. Compares the list of years to the dates of events.

Figure 3. Is a 'computer-generated' Julian calendar for the Roman month of April, in the year 34 A.D.

Figure 4. A side-by-side comparison of **incorrect** computer-generated calendars for the Passover months of Nisan and April.

Figure 5. A side-by-side comparison of **correct** computer-generated calendars for the Passover months of Nisan and April.

Figure 6. Overlap of the Day of Passover chart shows that Nisan 14 and April 22, 34 A.D. are the same day for 18 hours.

The U.S. Naval Observatory Findings[2]

The U.S. Naval Observatory Astronomical Applications Department ought to be a very reliable and unbiased source. Naval Oceanography Portal: The United States Naval Meteorology and Oceanography Command (NMOC) provides critical information from the ocean depths to the most distant reaches of space, meeting needs in the military, scientific, and civilian communities.

Chapter One Refresher

Here is a little refresher from Chapter One that will help to understand each column of the Naval Observatory's findings. All the dates and times given are according to the Roman year listed in **Column 1**. The Hebrew calendar year ends with the 'tekufah,' which we call the 'vernal equinox' (**Column 2**). According to Merriam-Webster, 'Equinox' descends from 'aequus,' the Latin word for 'equal,' and 'nox,' the Latin word for 'night'. A fitting history for a word that describes days of the year when the daytime and nighttime are equal in length. In the northern hemisphere, the vernal equinox marks the first day of spring and occurs when the sun moves north across the equator. ('*Vernal*' comes from the Latin word '*ver*,' meaning 'spring.')

The Hebrew calendar year <u>begins</u> with the first new moon appearance after the *tekufah* (**Columns 3**). The Jerusalem sighting of this first crescent (**Column 4**) could be a day or two after Column 3. That day, which is the next day (**Column 5**) becomes the first day of the first calendar month at evening. The fourteenth day of that month on the Hebrew calendar is Passover, but it starts the evening before the Roman date (**Column 6**). Note that it DOES NOT say the day before, which would be wrong; but rather the evening before- which is correct.

It is written: "In the fourteenth day of the first month at <u>evening</u> is the Lord's Passover" (Leviticus 23:5). Since the Hebrew month has either twenty-nine or thirty days, and Passover takes place on the fourteenth day of the month; it occurs when the moon is full, or almost full, because it is two weeks after the first appearance of the new moon.

The charts of Figure 2 on the next two pages show the findings of the United States Naval Observatory Astronomical Applications Department. The results of these findings will be explained once all the charts have been reviewed. The following astronomical data in the first three columns below was obtained from the U.S. Naval Observatory Astronomical Applications Department. The pertinent file can be accessed on the Internet at the following website. <u>http://aa.usno.navy.mil/data/docs/SpringPhenom.html.</u>
Note: The times of day given in the second and third columns have been adjusted +2 hours from U.S. Naval Observatory figures to account for the difference between *Jerusalem Israel* and *Greenwich England* (universal) time.
It should also be noted that the first evening of a visible crescent moon (**Column 4**) *always* occurs only minutes after sundown, which is at the very beginning of a new day on the Hebrew calendar. <u>This</u>

<u>Hebrew day correlates to the *following* day on the Julian calendar</u> as noted in the chart below (**Column 5**). **Column 6** is Passover dates for the given years. This is information as per the U.S. Naval Observatory Astronomical Applications Department.

The underlined statement above, which states: "This Hebrew day correlates to the *following* day on the Julian calendar" will be disputed in this chapter. Figure 5, developed later, gives the correct calendar and it will be shown why. All the calendars have been computer-generated.

FIGURE 2.[3]

Comparing the Years to the Events of the Other Five Columns
U.S. Naval Observatory Astronomical Applications Dept.

Column 1	Column 2	Column 3
Year	Vernal Equinox	Astronomical New Moon Conjunction (On date or first after vernal Equinox)
29 A.D.	Tues. Mar. 22, 6 p.m.	Sat. Apr. 2, 7 p.m.**
30 A.D.	Wed. Mar. 22, 0*	Wed. Mar. 22, 8 p.m.***
31 A.D.	Fri. Mar. 23, 5 a.m.	Tues. Apr. 10, 2 p.m.
32 A.D.	Sat. Mar. 22, 11 a.m.	Sat. Mar. 29, 10 p.m.**
33 A.D.	Sun. Mar. 22, 5 p.m.	Fri. Apr. 17, 9 p.m.**
34 A.D.	*Mon. Mar. 22, 11 p.m.*	*Wed. Apr. 7, 2 p.m.*
35 A.D.	Wed. Mar. 23, 5 a.m.	Mon. Mar. 28, 6 a.m.
36 A.D.	Thu. Mar. 22, 11 p.m.	Sun. Apr. 15, 5 a.m.
37 A.D.	Fri. Mar. 22, 4 p.m.	Thu. Apr. 4, noon

Figure 2. Col.1,2,3

* Midnight at the end of the given day.

** Conjunction occurs too late in the day for crescent to be seen from Jerusalem the next evening.

*** Conjunction occurred *on* date of Equinox actually preceding it by 4 hours. But as noted above, it is the <u>*visible*</u> crescent that established the 1st of Nisan which occurred on the 2nd evening *after* Equinox.

(Figure 2. includes Columns 2 thru 6 as they compare to Column 1.)

FIGURE 2. (Continued)

Column 1	Column 4	Column 5
Year	First evening of visible crescent	Date of the first of Nisan
29 A.D.	Mon. Apr. 4	Tues. Apr. 5
30 A.D.	Fri. Mar. 24	Sat. Mar. 25
31 A.D.	Wed. Apr. 11	Thurs. Apr. 12
32 A.D.	Mon. Mar. 31	Tues. Apr. 1
33 A.D.	Sun. Apr. 19	Mon. Apr. 20
34 A.D.	*Thurs. Apr. 8*	*Fri. Apr. 9*
35 A.D.	Tues. Mar. 29	Wed. Mar. 30
36 A.D.	Mon. Apr. 16	Tues. Apr. 17
37 A.D.	Fri. Apr. 5	Sat. Apr. 6

Figure 2. Col.1,4,5

Column 1	Column 6
Year	14th day of Nisan (Passover)
29 A.D.	Mon. Apr. 18
30 A.D.	Fri. Apr. 7
31 A.D.	Wed. Apr. 25
32 A.D.	Mon. Apr. 14
33 A.D.	Sun. May 3
34 A.D.	*Thurs. Apr. 22*
35 A.D.	Tues. Apr. 12
36 A.D.	Mon. Apr. 30
37 A.D.	Fri. Apr. 19

Figure 2. Col.1,6

Figure 2 tells us that the vernal equinox occurred on Monday, March 22nd at 11 p.m. in the year 34 A.D. on the Julian calendar. (This is +2hrs from Greenwich England time, GMT). The first or near new moon after the vernal equinox occurred on Wednesday, April 7th at 2 p.m. That new moon would then be sighted the next day in Jerusalem on Thursday, April 8th. The day after that first sighting, Friday, the 9th of April, would then be the first day of the first month of the Hebrew calendar year; and it becomes the 1st of Nisan. Thirteen days later, Nisan 14, at 6 p.m. would be Passover. This would fall on the 22nd of April on the Julian calendar.

Note the use of the terms Julian calendar and Gregorian calendars. Both are terms that are used for the Roman calendar, but they came into existence at different times in history. The Julian calendars are as of 46 B.C. and the Gregorian as of 1582.[4] For simplicity sake, this commentary will just use the term 'Julian calendar' for that is the one that applies. It should also be noted that Passover for the year 35 A.D. is Tuesday April 12th, and the year 36 A.D. has it as Monday, April 30th, therefore neither would be an actual Thursday Passover from which to choose.

The following pages will confirm a Thursday, April 22nd, 34 A.D. date in history for the Passover on which Jesus was crucified. Figure 3 depicts the Julian calendar of that year. It is derived from the information given in the six columns of Figure 2 that are according to Roman time.

FIGURE 3.
Calendar for April 34 A. D. (Julian Calendar)

Su	Mo	Tu	We	Th	Fr	Sa
				1	2	3
4	5	6	7	8	9	10
11	12	13	14	15	16	17
18	19	20	21	(22)	23	24
25	26	27	28	29	30	

Figure 3.

This is a representation of the Julian calendar for the month of April in the year 34 A.D., as obtained from the information in Figure 2. The 22nd is listed as Passover but is noted as starting at sundown the evening before on Nisan 14. Some would assume this to be the fourth day of the Jewish week. This is because the Roman day starts six hours after the Hebrew day. The months of the Hebrew and Julian calendars begin and end at different times. This leads to a problem for calendar makers. Because of the differing hours in which the days begin, they make the Hebrew day a day before the Roman day. Therefore, because of this discrepancy, the problem with a side-by-side comparison develops. This problem will be addressed next in Figure 4.

The Problem with Side-By-Side Calendar Comparisons

What is shown here corresponds to the year 3795[5] on the Hebrew calendar as created by calendar makers. It is the month of Nisan that begins the Hebrew ecclesiastical calendar year. Look at the side-by-side comparison below of the Hebrew and Julian calendars, which most calendar generators will give you. An effort will be made to try to explain this problem in more detail. The Julian calendar is determined first, and then the Hebrew is created as a day before.

Figure 4.

Incorrect Comparison of Calendars for Side-by-Side Months

NISAN							APRIL						
Days of the Week							Days of the Week						
1	2	3	4	5	6	7	Su	Mo	Tu	We	Th	Fr	Sa
											1	2	3
26	27	28	29	1	2	3	4	5	6	7	8	9	10
4	5	6	7	8	9	10	11	12	13	14	15	16	17
11	12	13	(14)	15	16	17	18	19	20	21	(22)	23	24
18	19	20	21	22	23	24	25	26	27	28	29	30	1
25	26	27	28	29	30	1	2	3	4	5	6	7	8
(Wrong)							(Correct)						

Figure 4.

The PROBLEM is that you cannot compare the calendars side by side, as shown in Figure 4 above. This is because the Hebrew calendar day begins only 6 hours before the Roman calendar day and not 24 hours, or a full day, as a side-by-side comparison appears to indicate. The overlap is not seen and can lead to a complete misunderstanding of dates such as Passover.

Even looking at the Hebrew calendar on the previous page, do not think of Passover as a day before because it is not. The fourteenth is placed as the fourth day because the calendar maker felt it had to begin a day before the fifth day of the week on the Roman calendar. First, the Jews do not use the Roman days of the weeks because they are taken from the names of Roman gods or planets. The Jews would never use such names. Over all these years they have kept to the Genesis account of an evening and a day as one day, and the use of calling those days simply the *first day*, the *second day*, etc., up to the *seventh day*, which is the day of the Sabbath rest. This is to say a 24-hour day is from evening to evening, (6 p.m. – 6 p.m.). Today most of the world does as the Romans did then; a 24-hour day that begins and ends at midnight.

Now people can dispute calendar years and dates all they want, how they originate, and all the different methods used, etc. But it does not matter, because without any effort and using only the scriptures we were able to come within a year or two. And then, to find a year that perfectly fits our personal findings is reassuring enough that this is indeed the correct answer.

It should be noted that some great minds, like Isaac Newton, have decided on a 34 A.D. crucifixion, but have chosen Friday, April 23rd as Passover, but never considers the three days and three nights prophecy of Jonah that Christ talked about. Remember the NMOC said: Hebrew day correlates to the *following* day on our Gregorian calendar. This means they would not place it as the same day since the Hebrew day started 6 hours earlier; therefore, it is put erroneously as the previous day on the Hebrew Calendar. This is incorrect, which is to say they should be depicted as the same day. They are not because of the six-hour time difference in a day, hence the problem with side-by-side comparisons.

Figures 5 and 6 to follow will show how the events of the day of Passover and of the crucifixion <u>are the same day</u> on both calendars and should not be displayed as a day apart. This is because for eighteen hours they are the very same day and that cannot be dismissed.

- Passover began at 6 p.m. on the fifth day of the Jewish week, Nisan 14.
- Six hours later the 22nd of April began at 12 a.m. on a Thursday (the fifth day of the Roman week).
- At 3 p.m. (the ninth hour of the 'day') of the fifth day of the Jewish week, Jesus died on the cross.

AND

- At 3 p.m. in the afternoon on Thursday, the 22nd of April, the fifth day of the Roman week, Jesus died on the cross.

Same day – Same time.

Figure 5.

Correct Calendar Comparison for Side-by-Side Months

NISAN								APRIL						
Days of the Week								Days of the Week						
1	2	3	4	5	6	7		Su	Mo	Tu	We	Th	Fr	Sa
												1	2	3
25	26	27	28	29	1	2		4	5	6	7	8	9	10
3	4	5	6	7	8	9		11	12	13	14	15	16	17
10	11	12	13	(14)	15	16		18	19	20	21	(22)	23	24
17	18	19	20	21	22	23		25	26	27	28	29	30	1
24	25	26	27	28	29	30		2	3	4	5	6	7	8
(Wrong)								(Correct)						

Figure 5.

Figure 6.

Overlap of the Hebrew/Roman Day of Passover

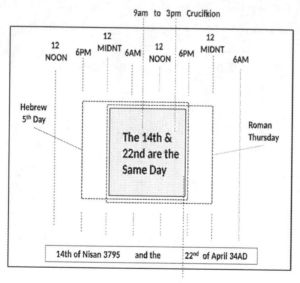

Figure 6.

It should be noted that the above chart shows that the 14th of Nisan is not a day before the 22nd of April. But in fact, eighteen out of the twenty-four hours, or three fourths of the time, it is the SAME DAY as the 22nd of April. It may be correct to calendar makers to determine the Julian Calendar Passover date and then make the Hebrew Calendar Passover date of Nisan 14 to be a day before. But that is what is confusing to the eye and to the reader, as shown here, and it is believed they are being created in error.

Jesus died on Passover, the fifth day of the Jewish week at 3 p.m. Which is also the same time and day, the fifth day or Thursday, of the Roman week, at 3 p.m. The Jewish date was Nisan 14 in the year 3795, and the Roman date was the 22nd of April, in the year 34 A.D.

Fact #7. The day of the crucifixion is the fifth day of the Jewish week, which would be our Thursday. This shows the answer of the seventh fact in Chapter One that states this very thing.

Next, we will look at how the days from the Passover to the Resurrection meet the requirements of what Jesus referred to as the Sign of the Prophet Jonah. This truth is necessary to fulfill and confirm the dating process just shown.

CHAPTER NINE

FULFILLING THE SIGN OF THE PROPHET JONAH

"For as Jonah was... so will the Son of Man be..."
(Matthew 12:40).

Jonah's *'Disobedience'* to God's Will

"And he (Jonah) said to them, "Pick me up and throw me into the sea. Then the sea will become calm for you, for I know that on account of me this great storm has come upon you" (Jonah 1:12).

"So, they picked up Jonah, threw him into the sea, and the sea stopped its raging" (Jonah 1:15).

"And the Lord appointed a great fish to swallow Jonah, and Jonah was in the stomach of the fish three days and three nights" (Jonah 1:17).

"Then Jonah prayed to the Lord his God from the stomach of the fish, and he said, "I cried out of my distress to the Lord, and He answered me. I cried for help from the depth of Sheol; You heard my voice" (Jonah 2:1, 2).

"Then the Lord commanded the fish, and it vomited Jonah up onto dry land" (Jonah 2:10).

Jesus' *'Obedience'* to God's Will

"Then some of the scribes and Pharisees said to Him, "Teacher, we want to see a sign from You." But He answered and said to them, "An evil and adulterous generation craves for a sign; and yet no sign will be given to it but the <u>sign of Jonah the prophet</u>; "For as Jonah was three days and three nights in the belly of the sea monster so will the <u>Son of Man be three days and three nights in the heart of the earth.</u> The men of Nineveh will stand up with this generation at the judgment and will condemn it because they repented at the preaching of Jonah; and behold, something greater than Jonah is here. The Queen of the South will rise up with this generation at the judgment and will condemn it, because she came from the ends of the earth to hear the wisdom of Solomon; and behold, something greater than Solomon is here" (Matthew 12:38-42).

Now that Jesus has said this, He must then fulfill every word He spoke; three days and three nights in the heart of the earth. Later He would be buried in a tomb for three days and three nights, and in that exact order. Jesus calls this, *the sign of Jonah the Prophet*, and it is necessary for Jesus to complete this sign to be the Son of Man as He claims. Therefore, an in-depth effort will be made to show exactly how Jesus did fulfill the sign of the prophet Jonah and the dating process used from the previous chapter. Here is a review of each day from Chapter Two as it relates to the sign of Jonah.

The Days Associated with the Sign of Jonah

Starting with Nisan 14 - The Day of Passover and the Day of the Crucifixion of Jesus Christ.

<u>Nisan 14</u>, - after the Crucifixion, but still the fifth day of the Jewish week, our Thursday.

"For as yet they did not understand the scripture, that He must rise again from the dead" (John 20:9). Before Jesus would rise bodily, His Spirit would first descend to 'Abraham's Bosom,' a portion of 'Hades,' where the spirits and souls of the righteous dead were held. Hades is the Old Testament 'Sheol.' This place is talked about in the story of the rich man and Lazarus found in Luke Chapter 16. The Psalmist said about Him, "For you will not abandon my soul to Sheol, nor will You allow Your Holy One to undergo decay" (Psalm 16:10). This is similar to what Jonah said, "I cried for help from the depth of Sheol; You heard my voice" (Jonah 2:2).

With Jesus being buried near the end of the day (put in the tomb), before evening came, this is the beginning of <u>the first day</u> of the three days and three nights according to the sign of Jonah. For any part of the next three days and three nights He descends to where the spirits and souls of the departed spirits were in Hades, as we saw here in these scriptures. (Please see the true story of the rich man and Lazarus, Luke 16:19-31).

<u>Nisan 15,</u> - one day after Passover, the sixth day of the Jewish week, our Friday

This is the first day of the Feast of Unleavened Bread, a High Sabbath day. A High Sabbath, and it is the first of two consecutive Sabbaths, as mentioned in John 19:31. The 'evening' of Nisan 15, which comes before the *day*, ends the first day at 6 p.m. and begins the first night of the three days and three nights according to the sign of Jonah.

This day was a high holy day, and these religious leaders were very active, instead of resting and worshipping. The scriptures say:

> Now on the next day, the day after the preparation,
> the chief priests and the Pharisees gathered together
> with Pilate, and said, "Sir, we remember that when He
> was still alive that deceiver said, 'After three days I
> am to rise again.' Therefore, give orders for the grave

to be made secure until the third day, otherwise His disciples may come and steal Him away and say to the people, 'He has risen from the dead,' and the last deception will be worse than the first." Pilate said to them, "You have a guard; go, make it as secure as you know how." And they went and made the grave secure, and along with the guard they set a seal on the stone (Matthew 27:62-66).

Then the daytime of Nisan15, which follows the evening, ends the first night at 6 a.m. and begins the second day according to the sign of Jonah the Prophet. It is necessary to remember that the evening precedes the daytime according to Jewish dating and timing.

Nisan 16, - two days after Passover, the seventh day of the Jewish week, our Saturday.

The second day of the Feast of Unleavened Bread was the normal weekly Sabbath. (Second of two Sabbaths, John 19:31 and Matthew 26:1) This evening ends the second day of the sign of Jonah and now begins the second night at 6 p.m. It is believed that during this day the women prepared the spices. "Then they returned and prepared spices and fragrant oils. And on the Sabbath, they rested according to the commandment" (Luke 23:56). The daylight hours of Nisan 16, following the evening, end the second night of the sign of Jonah and now begin the third day at 6 a.m.

Nisan 17, - three days after Passover, the first day of the Jewish week, our Sunday.

It is now the beginning of the third day of the Feast of Unleavened Bread. The evening of Nisan 17, at 6 p.m., is the end of the third day of the sign of Jonah and begins the third night. The day that follows the weekly Sabbath, after the Passover, would see the first fruits of the land and would signify the resurrection of Christ.

Sometime during the evening hours of Nisan 17, the first day of the week, Jesus would rise from the dead. With this Jesus would fulfill the sign of the prophet Jonah. As Jesus said, "<u>For as Jonah was three days and three nights in the belly of the sea monster, so will the Son of Man be three days and three nights in the heart of the earth</u>" (Matthew 12:40).

The coming of daylight on Nisan 17 becomes the <u>end of the third night</u> of the three days and three nights according to the sign of Jonah. With Jesus being risen before dawn, on what would be the fourth day (of sign of Jonah), He does not violate the three days and three nights of the sign of Jonah. To be sure, any day other than a fifth day of the week Passover/Crucifixion would violate this specific sign that Jesus gave- The Sign of Jonah the Prophet.

God made it possible that the Resurrection was on the first day of both the Hebrew and the Roman week.

The Resurrection worked out to be after the third night began and before the light of the next day according to the Roman week as well as the Hebrew week. This would have been sometime late Saturday night before dawn. Jesus would already be raised before daylight on the first day of the Hebrew and Roman week. Jesus was in the heart of the earth three days- Thursday (1) (even though partial), Friday (2) and Saturday (3); and three nights- Thursday night (1), Friday night (2) and Saturday night (3). Jesus answered them, "Destroy this temple and in three days I will raise it up" (John 2:19). Friday was in one day, Saturday was in two days and in three days, Sunday, He was raised, just as He said He would. Therefore, Sunday is the Lord's Day because that is the day the angel said He is not here (in the tomb) for HE IS RISEN.

Figure 7.

The Resurrection on the First Days of the Week

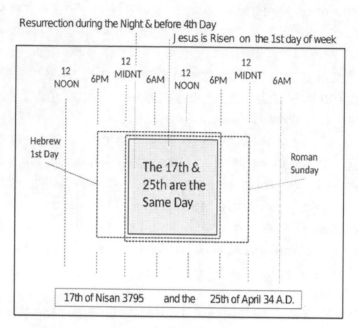

Resurrection during the Night & before 4th Day

Jesus is Risen on the 1st day of week

| 12 NOON | 6PM | 12 MIDNT | 6AM | 12 NOON | 6PM | 12 MIDNT | 6AM |

Hebrew 1st Day

Roman Sunday

The 17th & 25th are the Same Day

17th of Nisan 3795   and the   25th of April 34 A.D.

Figure 7.

Figure 7 shows how it works out that Jesus rose from the dead on the first day of the week on both the Hebrew and the Roman calendars. The main thing that was learned from the previous chapter was not to be confused by the dating systems.

To Summarize

The first way Jesus fulfilled the Sign of Jonah was according to the Hebrew Calendar:

> The Jewish Day is from 6 p.m. to 6 p.m.
> The 'Night' starts at 6 p.m. and lasts until 6 a.m.
> Then the 'Day' starts at 6 a.m. and lasts until 6 p.m.
> 12 hours dark, 12 hours light, equals a 24-hour day
> The Dark is Night, the Light is Day

"God called the light *day*, and the darkness he called *night*. And there was evening, and there was morning, one day" (Genesis 1:5).

Figure 8.

Crucifixion to the Resurrection for the month of Nisan

Weekday	Hour	Night/Day	Date	Sign of Jonah
5th	6 p.m.	N	14th	Last Supper
5th	6 a.m.	N	14th	Mock trial
5th	9 a.m.	D	14th	Jesus crucified
5th	12 p.m.	D	14th	Darkness
5th	3 p.m.	D	14th	Jesus Died
5th	3-6pm	D	14th	Jesus Buried
5th	3-6pm	D	14th	Begins 1st day
6th	6 p.m.	N	15th	End 1st Day
6th	6 p.m.	N	15th	Begins 1st Night
6th	6 a.m.	D	15th	Ends 1st Night
6th	6 a.m.	D	15th	Begins 2nd Day
7th	6 p.m.	N	16th	End 2nd Day
7th	6 p.m.	N	16th	Begins 2nd Night
7th	6 a.m.	D	16th	End 2nd Night
7th	6 a.m.	D	16th	Begins 3rd Day
1st	6 p.m.	N	17th	End 3rd Day
1st	6 p.m.	N	17th	Begins 3rd Night
1st	12 a.m.	N	17th	Dark Hours
1st	12-6am	N	17th	Resurrection
1st	6 a.m.	D	17th	Jesus seen Alive
1st	6 a.m.	D	17th	End 3rd Night
2nd	6 p.m.	N	18th	Seen by Disciples

Figure 8.

What follows on this page is a second way of looking at how Jesus fulfilled the sign of Jonah according to the Hebrew calendar.

Nisan 14, Passover is the fifth Day of Jewish Week

- Jesus crucified 9 a.m., died at 3 p.m.
- Jesus removed from the cross before Sabbaths began
- Buried before 6 p.m. on fifth day of the week
- Begins first Day of Sign of Jonah at 3 p.m.

<u>Nisan 15, is the first day of Feast of Unleavened Bread</u>

- Ends First Day of Sign of Jonah at 6 p.m.
- First Night of Sign of Jonah starts at 6 p.m. to 6 a.m.
- A High Sabbath, sixth Day of Jewish Week
- Ends first night of Sign of Jonah at 6 a.m.
- Second Day of Sign of Jonah starts at 6 a.m. to 6 p.m.

<u>Nisan16, is the second day of Feast of Unleavened Bread</u>

- Ends Second Day of Sign of Jonah at 6 p.m.
- Second Night of the Sign of Jonah starts at 6 p.m. to 6 a.m.
- Seventh Day of Week, regular weekly Sabbath
- Third Day of the Sign of Jonah starts at 6 a.m. to 6 p.m.
- Ends second Night of Sign of Jonah at 6 a.m.

<u>Nisan 17, is the third day of Feast of Unleavened Bread</u>

- Ends third Day of Sign of Jonah at 6 p.m.
- Third Night of the Sign of Jonah starts at 6 p.m.
- First Day of the Week, after Sabbaths, starts at 6 p.m.
- Jesus Resurrected before the light of day (6 a.m.)
- Ends third night of Sign of Jonah at 6 a.m.
- Jesus fulfills the sign of Jonah being in the heart of the earth three days and three nights.

To Summarize (continued)

Here is how Jesus fulfilled the Sign of Jonah according to the <u>Roman (Julian) Calendar</u>:

Roman Day from 12 a.m. to 12 a.m.
The 'Day' starts at 6 a.m. and lasts until 6 p.m.
Then the 'Night' starts at 6 p.m. and lasts until 6 a.m.

6 hours dark, 12 hours light, 6 hours dark.

The Dark is Night, the Light is Day

"God called the light 'day,' and the darkness He called 'night'..." (Genesis 1:5). But the Romans did not go by the Genesis account of a day, they used 12 a.m. to 12 a.m. as one 24-hour day.

The 22nd of April 34 A.D. Passover – a Thursday

- Jesus dies on the cross at 3 p.m.
- Jesus removed from the cross before Sabbaths began
- Jesus buried shortly after 3 p.m. on Thursday
- Begin first Day of Sign of Jonah shortly after 3 p.m.
- End first Day of Sign of Jonah at 6 p.m.
- Begin first Night of Sign of Jonah at 6 p.m. to 6 a.m.
- The 22nd ends at 12 a.m.

The 23rd of April is Friday of Roman Week

- The 23rd begins at 12 a.m.
- End first Night of Sign of Jonah at 6 a.m.
- Begin second Day of sign of Jonah at 6 a.m. to 6 p.m.
- End second Day of Sign of Jonah at 6 p.m.
- Begin second Night of Sign of Jonah at 6 p.m. to 6 a.m.

The 24th of April is Saturday of Roman Week

- The 24th begins at 12 a.m.
- End second Night of Sign of Jonah at 6 a.m.
- Begins third Day of Sign of Jonah at 6 a.m. to 6 p.m.
- Ends third Day of Sign of Jonah at 6 p.m.
- Begins third Night of Sign of Jonah at 6 p.m. to 6 a.m.

The 25th of April is Sunday of Roman Week

- The 25th begins at 12 a.m.
- Begins first Day of the week at 12 a.m.
- Jesus resurrected while it was still dark, before 6 a.m.
- Ends third Night of Sign of Jonah at 6 a.m.
- Jesus declared to be risen by the angel after dawn
- Jesus is resurrected on the first day of the week
- Jesus appears to the disciples the evening of the first day of the week, after 6 p.m.

Jesus fulfills the sign of Jonah according to Jewish and Roman time, and in the specific order of three days and three nights as required. To confirm these findings: Thursday (the fifth weekday), though a partial day, counts as the first day. Friday (the sixth weekday) is the first night and the second day. Saturday (the seventh weekday) is the second night and the third day. Sunday (the first weekday) is the third night, whereby Jesus rose before dawn. The prophecy was, "For as Jonah was three days and three nights in the belly of the sea monster, so will the Son of Man be three days and three nights in the heart of the earth" (Matthew 12:40).

If Thursday (the fifth day) is not the first day, then the first night would come before the first day, and that cannot be. There is no time of day given, or part of a day, that Jonah was swallowed up or spewed out of that great fish. Therefore, this method of dating is fine. The day Jonah was swallowed is the first day, as is the day Jesus went into the tomb the first day. The night that Jonah was spewed out of the great fish is the third night, as the night Jesus rose from the grave is also the third night. Jesus was not seen by anyone until daylight came on the first day of the week. That day the angel announced, after the fact, that He is not here (in the tomb), 'He is Risen.' It fits on the Hebrew calendar as well as the Roman calendar in the year 34 A.D.

A <u>Wednesday Passover</u> does not work

According to Hebrew calendar, a 24-hour day is from 6 p.m. to 6 p.m.

A new day begins at 6 p.m. (in the evening)

The <u>N</u>ight is from 6 p.m. to 6 a.m.

Then the <u>D</u>ay is from 6 a.m. to 6 p.m.

The fourth day of the week would be Wednesday

- The fourth weekday at 3 p.m. (Jesus buried) to the fourth weekday at 6 p.m. is first Day of the sign of Jonah
- The fifth weekday at 6 p.m. to the fifth weekday at 6 a.m. is the first Night of the sign of Jonah
- The fifth weekday at 6 a.m. to the fifth weekday at 6 p.m. is the second Day of the sign of Jonah
- The sixth weekday at 6 p.m. to the sixth weekday at 6 a.m. is the second Night of the sign of Jonah
- The sixth weekday at 6 a.m. to the sixth weekday at 6 p.m. is the third Day of the sign of Jonah
- The seventh weekday at 6 p.m. to the seventh weekday at 6 a.m. is the third Night of the sign of Jonah
- The seventh weekday at 6 a.m. to the seventh weekday at 6 p.m. is the fourth Day of the sign of Jonah
- The first weekday at 6 p.m. to the first weekday at 6 a.m. is the fourth Night of the sign of Jonah

In order for the resurrection to be on the first day of the week Jesus would have to rise on the fourth night before 6 a.m. This violates the sign of the prophet Jonah. The year 31 A.D. is the closest year that has a Wednesday Passover. This also does not fall within the probable timeline for the crucifixion that has been determined as between 32 A.D. and 36 A.D.

A <u>Friday Passover</u> does not work either

According to Hebrew calendar, a 24-hour day is from 6 p.m. to 6 p.m.
A new day begins at 6 p.m. (in the evening)
The <u>N</u>ight is from 6 p.m. to 6 a.m.
Then the <u>D</u>ay is from 6 a.m. to 6 p.m.
Friday would be the sixth day of the week

- The sixth weekday at 3 p.m. (Jesus buried) to the sixth weekday at 6 p.m. is the first Day of the sign of Jonah
- The seventh weekday at 6 p.m. to the seventh weekday at 6 a.m. is the first Night of the sign of Jonah
- The seventh weekday at 6 a.m. to the seventh weekday at 6 p.m. is the second Day of the sign of Jonah
- The first weekday at 6 p.m. to the first weekday at 6 a.m. is the second Night of the sign of Jonah
- The first weekday at 6 a.m. to the first weekday at 6 p.m. is the third Day of the sign of Jonah
- The second weekday at 6 p.m. to the second weekday at 6 a.m. is the third Night of the sign of Jonah

In order for the resurrection to be on the first day of the week Jesus would have to rise on the second night before 6 a.m. This violates the sign of the prophet Jonah. The year 30 A.D. is the closest year that has a Friday Passover. This also does not fall within the probable timeline for the crucifixion that has been determined as between 32 A.D. and 36 A.D.

Jesus rose from the dead between 12 p.m. and 6 a.m. on our Sunday, the first day of the Jewish week also. The date was April 25th 34 A.D. on the Roman Calendar and Nisan 17 on the Hebrew calendar. Jesus is who He says He is and has fulfilled all that He has declared about Himself, especially the reasons for His coming, as will be shown next.

CHAPTER TEN

FULFILLING THE REASONS FOR HIS COMING

"The Son of God appeared for this purpose…" (1 John 3:8).

What the Scripture say about why Jesus came

There were many other meticulous and marvelous details about the life of Christ that needed to be explored for Jesus to be the Passover Lamb. These too were necessary to fulfill the Passover feast, and the types and shadows that were representative of it. The importance goes beyond fulfilling and ending the Passover obligations. It goes beyond Jesus' defeat of principalities and powers, and beyond overcoming the grave and Hell by His death, burial and resurrection. Jesus also fulfilled the very reasons for His coming, which went beyond Passover.

It will now be shown why this is so necessary to our understanding. It is believed all of history prior to this event looked forward to that one particular Passover Day. Now all of time since then has looked back to that Passover Day. It is the day that has changed everything thing for all time.

JESUS SAID HE CAME FOR THREE PARTICULAR REASONS – ALL OF WHICH WERE FULFILLED BEGINNING ON THAT SPECIAL PASSOVER DAY.

To Give His Life as a Ransom

The First of which was to give His life as a ransom.

"For even the Son of Man did not come to be served, but to serve, and to give His life as a ransom for many" (Mark 10:45 and Matthew 20:28).

"For there is one God, and one mediator also between God and men, the man Christ Jesus, who gave Himself as a ransom for all, the testimony given at the proper time" (1 Timothy 2:5, 6).

This was the plan of God from the beginning of time, or before, and to this testimony is given. Jesus is the Lamb slain from the foundation of the world (Revelation 13:8). God knew that man would fall and was not caught off guard or surprised by their actions in the garden. He had a plan already in place where He would send His Son, His incarnate self, to be a ransom for the sins of mankind. A plan so awesome that it would prove the complete and utter love of God for His most precious creation.

That Passover Day is when His plan would find its fulfillment. The high priest, Caiaphas, was right when he said it was necessary that one man die for the people (John 18:14). Jesus said no man takes His life from Him, rather He willingly lays it down (John 10:18). The wages of sin is death (Romans 6:23), and the evidence of the high cost of sin is that all men since Adam have died (1 Corinthians 15:22). Now all must be redeemed from this curse of sin and from death's sting. The scriptures say without the shedding of blood there is no forgiveness of sins (Hebrews 9:22), for the life is in the blood (Leviticus 17:11).

The high priest could not offer the lamb sacrifice for the sins of the people until he first made an offering for himself, for he too was sinful (Hebrews 7:27). The blood of bulls and goats was insufficient because they could not cleanse a man's conscience and the daily offering was itself a reminder of one's own sinfulness (Hebrews 10:4).

It would take an offering of a High Priest after the order of Melchizedek (Hebrew 7:17), a King of Peace, one who had neither beginning nor end. It would take One not born of man, but One who would be the seed of the woman (Genesis 3:15) and born of a virgin (Isaiah 7:14). One who would take on human flesh and be touched with the feelings of all our infirmities. Yet He Himself would be without sin (Hebrews 4:15).

Yes, the wages of sin are death, but the gift of God is eternal life through Jesus Christ (Romans 6:23). Jesus gave His life in exchange for our sin debt. It was while we were yet sinners that Christ died for us (Romans 5:8). Now we are bought with a price (1 Corinthians 6:20), for He paid the ransom for our very souls. His death in exchange for our lives! He who knew no sin became sin for us, that we might become the righteousness of God in Christ (2 Corinthians 5:21). Sin has no more dominion over us (Romans 6:14) and now there is no longer fear in death, for death has lost its sting. Perfect love has cast out all fear, thanks be to God (1 John 4:18). Like a lamb to the slaughter (Isaiah 53:7), Christ our Passover sacrificed for us (1 Corinthians 5:7) on that Passover Day. The RANSOM has been paid!

To Destroy the Works of the Devil

The Second reason was to destroy the works of the devil.

"The one who practices sin is of the devil, for the devil has sinned from the beginning. The Son of God appeared for this purpose, to destroy the works of the devil" (1 John 3:8).

What were those works? Well to begin with it was that old serpent, the devil, which tempted and deceived Adam and Eve in the garden to disobey God. The result was the curse upon all God's creation (Genesis 3:17 and Isaiah 24:6). The sinful nature of the first man is passed on to all mankind, and all need redeemed (Romans 3:23). Mankind has been blinded by sin and has made everything to be all about him.

A rebellion would also take place in heaven giving way to demonic spirits that followed Satan and were likewise cast down to earth with him (2 Peter 2:4). The works also included those who were bound by evil spirits from whom Jesus was casting them out (Matthew 8:16). Jesus would also heal the sick, open blind eyes, cause the lame to walk and the deaf to hear (Matthew 15:30).

Yes, to destroy the works of the devil just as He said. And when you, being dead in your trespasses and in the uncircumcision of your flesh, He made you alive together with Him, having forgiven your all trespasses (Colossians 2:13). He has wiped out the handwriting of requirements that were against us and which were contrary to us. He has taken it out of the way, having nailed it to the cross- on Passover. Having disarmed principalities and powers, He made a public spectacle of them, triumphing over them (Colossians 2:14, 15) by the cross. Jesus has destroyed the works of the devil!

When did all this happen? It happened on that Day of Passover as God's Passover Lamb hung crucified on Calvary's cross. By paying the ransom, Jesus has freed us from being a slave to sin to now being servants of righteousness (Romans 6:18). Then by destroying the works of the devil God has delivered us from the kingdom of darkness into the kingdom of His dear Son (Colossians 1:13).

Truly, greater is He who is in you than he who is in the world (1 John 4:4).

That We Would Have Abundant Life

The Third reason was that we might have life and have it more abundantly.

"The thief (devil) comes only to steal, and to kill and to destroy. I (Jesus) came that they might have life and have it more abundantly" (John 10:10). How is this even possible? First, because Jesus is the 'Good Shepherd' and we are the sheep of His pasture (John 10:11-14). He cares for His sheep and will not flee when trouble comes, for He has promised to never leave us nor forsake us (Hebrews 13:5). He knows all His sheep by name, and they know His voice (John 10:27). He leads His sheep in and out, so that they may find good pasture. His love for them is so overwhelming that He lays down His life for His sheep (John 15:13), and He has power to take it up again (John 10:18). So, the Lord is our Shepherd, just as Psalm 23 says, and surely goodness and mercy shall follow us all the days of our lives- That is Abundant Life.

Jesus also kept reminding His disciples that He must go away; in fact, it was to their, and our, advantage that He go away (John 16:7). Why? Because two, Jesus would pray to the Father and He would give us another Helper, that would abide with us forever- the Spirit of Truth (John 16:13). It is He whom the world cannot receive because it neither sees Him nor knows Him, for He dwells with you and shall be in you (John 14:17). This Helper, the Holy Spirit, whom the Father will send in Jesus' name, He will teach you all things, and bring to your remembrance all things that Jesus said (John 14:16). When the Helper comes, whom Jesus shall send to you from the Father, the Spirit of Truth who proceeds from the Father, He will testify of Jesus.

When the Spirit comes, He will convict the world of sin, and of righteousness, and of judgment (John 16:8). However, when He, the Spirit of Truth, has come, He will guide <u>you</u> into all truth; for He will not speak on His own authority, but whatever He hears He will speak;

and He will tell you things to come (John 16:13). He will glorify Jesus, for He will take of what is His and declare it to you.

Need any more be said? Having life and having it more abundantly is having the Holy Spirit dwell with us and in us; constantly showing us the things of Christ and bringing to our remembrance all that He has said and done. He will show us the truth of what is and what is to come. Though He brings conviction upon the world He brings comfort and confidence to the believers. This could not happen until Jesus went away, then it was a guaranteed promise to us (Romans 4:16).

Greater is He, the Holy Spirit, who is in you (1 John 4:4). When was this accomplished? When the Good Shepherd laid down His life for the sheep on Passover and was raised up three days later. He was and is both the Lamb of God and the Great Shepherd. He said, because I live you shall live also (John 14:19). That does not mean just existing, but living an abundant, Spirit directed life now and through eternity to come. Thank you, Jesus! Jesus came for these three reasons as He said, and He fulfilled each one, of course.

Jesus is now the Lamb of God in Heaven

Looking into the Book of Revelation, this truth unfolds as the Holy Spirit reveals heavenly things. What is seen in heaven? Listen as the Apostle John describes Jesus as the LAMB in heaven.

"And I saw between the throne (with the four living creatures) and the elders a LAMB standing, as if SLAIN, having seven horns and seven eyes, which are the seven Spirits of God, sent out into all the earth" (Revelation 5:6). "...The four living creatures and the twenty-four elders fell down before the LAMB..." (Revelation 5:8).

> Then I looked, and I heard the voice of many angels around the throne and the living creatures and

the elders; and the number of them was myriads of myriads, and thousands of thousands, saying with a loud voice, "Worthy is the LAMB that was SLAIN to receive power and riches and wisdom and might and honor and glory and blessing." And every created thing which is in heaven and on the earth and under the earth and on the sea, and all things in them, I heard saying, "To Him who sits on the throne, and to the LAMB, be blessing and honor and glory and dominion forever and ever" (Revelation 5:11-13).

"...These who are clothed in the white robes, who are they, and where have they come from?" "...These are the ones who come out of the great tribulation, and they have washed their robes and made them white in the BLOOD OF THE LAMB" (Revelation 7:13, 14).

Now the salvation, and the power, and the kingdom of our God and the authority of His Christ have come, for the accuser of our brethren has been thrown down, he who accuses them before our God day and night. And they overcame him because of the BLOOD OF THE LAMB and because of the word of their testimony, and they did not love their life even when faced with death.
(Revelation 12:10, 11).

Please excuse the lengthy detail, but it was to let the reader see the great effort that the Holy Spirit put upon the revelation of Jesus in heaven as the LAMB, above everything else. And the Lamb is the reference to the Passover Lamb of God sacrificed for us to take away the sin of the world. All of which was completed on that one special Passover Day as Passover was fulfilled. It was on the cross, on Passover, that Jesus said, "It is finished."

Jesus is referred to by many names in the Book of Revelation. These names include the Root of David, the Bright and Morning Star, the Alpha and the Omega, the First and the Last, Faithful and True, and- the Word of God.

> *There is only one name and one description that is consistent from Revelation Chapter Five through Chapter Twenty-Two: THE LAMB.*

To understand the great importance of the Passover fulfillment is to know and appreciate that Jesus is, in the Book of Revelation, consistently presented in heaven as the LAMB. From the time that Jesus rose from the dead it was not about Passover anymore, it was only about the LAMB.

It is the Lamb who is worshiped and bowed before around the throne. It is the Lamb who is worthy and who opens the seals (Revelation 5:12). It is the blood of the Lamb that makes white the robes of the saints (Revelation 7:14). It is the Lamb who the kings of the earth make war with and it is the Lamb that overcomes them (Revelation 17:14). It is the wife of the Lamb and the marriage supper of the Lamb that is celebrated (Revelation 19:9). It is the Lamb who is the temple and the light thereof (Revelation 21:23). And finally, it is the LAMB'S Book of Life in Revelation 21:27.

Does the reader see it and understand the importance of that Passover and what the fulfillment by Jesus Christ as the Lamb of God meant for all eternity? Grasp it and let His humility, and the redemption that He provided, for the sins of all men for all time- on that Passover day, change all of our lives forever. The Bible tells us we were dead in our trespasses and sins (Ephesians 2:1-5). But, based upon Jesus' words, "because I live, you will live also" (John 14:19), we have eternal life.

There is still one more reason Jesus came, and that is to fulfill the Law and the Prophets. The next section will show us how that is so, and it may not be what you expected or could have predicted.

CHAPTER ELEVEN

THE LAW AND PROPHETS FULFILLED

*"The law and the prophets were
until John..." (Luke 16:16).*

The Early Church

After the church was born it continued to mainly focus its attention on those in Jerusalem. This was in spite of what Jesus said in Matthew 28:20, that they were to go into all the world and make disciples of all men, teaching them to observe all that was commanded and baptizing them. This was to start with Judea, then Samaria and then to continue to reach outward.

Eventually it was Saul of Tarsus that persecuted the believers and caused havoc for the church. Although this persecution had come, the apostles and many new disciples still were not going into the entire world as they should have. The question is, did they know or fully understand what the commands and demands of them were? It is thought that they really did not understand because everything was so new and different to their centuries of traditions and practice. Even after Pentecost they struggled to get things right.

When one reads the New Testament, you find out something about the most religious of the times. They, the Scribes and

Pharisees, were more concerned about not doing what the law said not to do, than doing what was righteously required. Even the new converts struggled with aspects of the law. Until the conversion of the Apostle Paul the church was still trying to find its way as the Spirit gave direction. Understandably, that direction was up against thousands of years of Jewish law and tradition. What was common is that the new Jewish believer would want to become more committed to keeping the law as never before, thinking this is what is naturally pleasing to God. They in turn would make an effort to proselyte Gentiles to do likewise.

This section will show us that this way of thinking is not what God had in mind for the new believer and His church. It was shown how zealousness for the law on that Passover day led the religious leaders to falsely accuse One whom they thought would endanger their power and position with the people. This was to the point that they would not enter Pilate's palace with their false accusations and with a call for Christ's crucifixion. This was so they would not defile themselves and could keep holy the Passover. This hypocrisy of the deeply religious elite was addressed in detail by Jesus in the four gospels as He warned that all those who would do such things were in danger of hell's fire.

The New Testament will show how this zealousness for the law continued to the detriment of the church. The church had a new commandment now, which was to love one another, and against which there is no law. Here is one of the reasons this is so important. In Chapter Eight it was said Jesus came for three reasons, but there is a fourth that cannot be over-looked. Jesus said, "Do not think that I came to abolish the Law or the Prophets, I did not come to abolish but to fulfill" (Matthew 5:17). All that had been spoken about Jesus in types and shadows, in prophecy, and in those things concerning the law- from His birth through His resurrection, have been fulfilled. Jesus lived under the law, but He never violated the law. Only Jesus fulfilled the law. He alone has done it! Jesus has fulfilled all. Now He says...

To the Disciples

...you have heard it said... but I say (Matthew 5).

Early in Jesus' ministry He began to tell everyone that *you have heard it said, but I say.* This Jesus would say about things written in the law or spoken by the prophets. Meaning there is the letter of the law and then there is the spirit of the law.

> "You have heard that the ancients were told, "You shall not commit murder" and "Whoever commits murder shall be liable to the court." But I say to you that everyone who is angry with his brother shall be guilty before the court..." (Matthew 5:21, 22)."Again, you have heard that the ancients were told, "You shall not make false vows, but shall fulfill your vows to the Lord." But I say to you, make no oath at all..." (Matthew 5:33, 34). But let your statement be, Yes, yes, or No, no; anything beyond these is of evil" (Matthew 5:37). "You have heard that it was said, You shall love your neighbor and hate your enemy. But I say to you, love your enemies, and pray for those who persecute you..." (Matthew 5:43, 44).

Jesus was preparing His disciples and followers for the time when the first covenant (the law plus all the religious traditions) would end, as far as 'for righteousness' was concerned. It was satisfied and fulfilled, thus bringing its fleshy requirements to an end. Because Jesus said that He did not come to destroy the law; this meant that the spirit of the law still needed to be adhered to. This is the part where Jesus said, "But I say," -that part is what the believer is to be mindful of and must adhere to.

The biggest shocker of this reality is the encounter of Jesus with the Samaritan woman. There it was necessary to face the issue of where the place of worship would be in the future. It has always been the Jerusalem temple and one would obviously think this would continue to be so. What Jesus would say must have been hard for most to believe that it would ever be true.

The necessity of Temple worship

... the end to a designated place of worship (John 4).

"Jesus said to her (the Samaritan woman), "Woman, believe Me, an hour is coming when neither in this mountain, nor in Jerusalem will you worship the Father. You worship what you do not know; we worship what we know, for salvation is from the Jews. But an hour is coming, and now is, when the true worshipers will worship the Father in spirit and truth; for such people the Father seeks to be His worshipers. God is Spirit, and those who worship Him must worship in spirit and truth" (John 4:21-24).

Now the early church struggled with understanding two issues of the day. The first was the ever-present danger of religion itself, and the other was the revised call for the just to live by faith. There needed to be a revelation that the old covenant was done, and that a new covenant had come. Here are some excerpts from the Book of Hebrews showing the end of many of these demands of the law, of the old covenant.

To the Hebrews

... the end of Levitical priesthood (Hebrews 7).

"Now if perfection was through the Levitical priesthood (for on the basis of it the people received the Law), what further need was there for another priest to arise according to the order of Melchizedek, and not be designated according to the order of Aaron" (Hebrews 7:11)? "And inasmuch as it was not without an oath (for they indeed became priests without an oath, but He with an oath through the One who said to Him, "The Lord has sworn and will not change His mind, You are a priest forever") so much more Jesus has become the **guarantee of a better covenant**" (Hebrews 7:20-22).

... the end of the Old (first) Covenant (Hebrews 8).

"For if that first covenant had been faultless, there would have been no occasion sought for a second. For finding fault with them, He says: "Behold, days are coming, says the Lord, when I will effect a new covenant with the house of Israel and with the house of Judah" (Hebrews 8:7, 8).

"When He said, "A new covenant," **He has made the first obsolete**. But whatever is becoming obsolete and growing old is ready to disappear" (Hebrews 8:13).

... the end of Sacrifice and Offerings (Hebrews 10).

"After saying above, "Sacrifice and offering, and whole burnt offerings and sacrifices for sin You have not desired, nor have You taken pleasure in them" (which are offered according to the law), then He said, "Behold, I have come to do Your will." **He takes away the first in order to establish the second.** By this will we have been sanctified through the offering of the body of Jesus Christ once for all" (Hebrews 10:8-10).

... the end of any thoughts of justification by works (Hebrews 11).

"And without faith it is impossible to please Him, for he who comes to God must believe that He is, and that He is a rewarder of those who seek Him" (Hebrews 11:6).

Having seen from this one book the changes that Christ has brought about through His life, death and resurrection, shows what is to be an end to the bondage of adherence to the law of sin and death, and the newfound liberty of the Spirit of the law of love and life.

It was the unbelieving Jews that came after Paul, just as they did Jesus, to silence his message. There are other Books of the Bible that show how the believing Jews struggled with letting go of their Old Covenant to the point they were called Judaizers.[1] This meant they were trying to get new believers to hold to the Old Covenant, which includes the works of the law.

To the Messianic Jew

> ... myriads of believing Jews... zealous for the law (Acts 21).

"After we arrived in Jerusalem, the brethren received us gladly. And the following day Paul went in with us to James, and all the elders were present. After he had greeted them, he began to relate one by one the things which God had done among the Gentiles through his ministry. And when they heard it they began glorifying God; and they said to him, "You see, brother, how many thousands there are among the Jews of those who have believed, and they are all zealous for the Law; and they have been told about you, that you are teaching all the Jews who are among the Gentiles to forsake Moses, telling them not to circumcise their children nor to walk according to the customs" (Acts 21:17-21).

To Would be Teachers

> ... having strayed... desiring to be teachers of the law (1 Timothy 1).

"But the goal of our instruction is love from a pure heart and a good conscience and a sincere faith. For some men, straying from these things, have turned aside to fruitless discussion, wanting to be teachers of the Law, even though they do not understand either what they are saying or the matters about which they make confident assertions. But we know that the Law is good, if one uses it lawfully, realizing the fact that law is not made for a righteous person, but for those who are lawless and rebellious, for the ungodly and sinners, for the unholy and profane..." (1 Timothy 1:5-9).

To Would be Leaders

... hypocrisy of some early church leadership (Galatians Chapters 2 through 6).

> "But when Cephas came to Antioch, I opposed him to his face, because he stood condemned. For prior to the coming of certain men from James, he used to eat with the Gentiles; but when they came, he began to withdraw and hold himself aloof, fearing the party of the circumcision. The rest of the Jews joined him in hypocrisy, with the result that even Barnabas was carried away by their hypocrisy. But when I saw that they were not straightforward about the truth of the gospel..." (Galatians 2:11-14).

> "Nevertheless, knowing that a man is not justified by the works of the Law but through faith in Christ Jesus, even we have believed in Christ Jesus, so that we may be justified by faith in Christ and not by the works of the law, since by the works of the Law no flesh will be justified" (Galatians 2:16).

"Behold I, Paul, say to you that if you receive circumcision, Christ will be of no benefit to you. And I testify again to every man who receives circumcision that he is under obligation to keep the whole Law. You have been severed from Christ, you who are seeking to be justified by law; you have fallen from grace. For we through the Spirit, by faith, are waiting for the hope of righteousness. For in Christ Jesus neither circumcision nor uncircumcision means anything, but faith working through love" (Galatians 5:2-6).

"Those who desire to make a good showing in the flesh try to compel you to be circumcised, simply so that they will not be persecuted for the cross of Christ" (Galatians 6:12).

To the Value of Circumcision

... even circumcision is nothing (1 Corinthians 7).

"...And so I direct in all the churches. Was any man called when he was already circumcised? He is not to become uncircumcised. Has anyone been called in uncircumcision? He is not to be circumcised. Circumcision is nothing, and uncircumcision is nothing, but what matters is the keeping of the commandments of God" (1 Corinthians 7:17-19). "For we are the true circumcision, who worship in the Spirit of God and glory in Christ Jesus and put no confidence in the flesh" (Philippians 3:3).

To the Value of Observances

... the end of unnecessary observances (Colossians 2).

Therefore no one is to act as your judge in regard to food or drink or in respect to a festival or a new moon or a Sabbath day— things which are a mere shadow of what is to come; but the substance belongs to Christ (Colossians 2:16, 17). If you have died with Christ to the elementary principles of the world, why, as if you were living in the world, do you submit yourself to decrees, such as, "Do not handle, do not taste, do not touch!" (which all refer to things destined to perish with use)— in accordance with the commandments and teachings of men? These are matters which have, to be sure, the appearance of wisdom in self-made religion and self-abasement and severe treatment of the body but are of no value against fleshly indulgence (Colossians 2:20-23).

Those being referred to in these scriptures were being judged (by non-believing Jews and Judaizers) for NOT observing or being concerned about what they would eat or drink. They did not observe feast days or new moons and were NOT concerned about observing all the do not touch, taste or handle religious rites. Their new-found liberties of the Spirit meant that whatever they did or did not do was based on faith.

Yes, even the Sabbath

... an end to the 7th day Sabbath rest (Colossians 2).

(Repeating) "Therefore no one is to act as your judge in regard to food or drink or in respect to a festival or a new moon or a Sabbath day— things which are a mere shadow of what is to come; but the substance belongs to Christ" (Colossians 2:16, 17).

Again, as previously stated, this judgment is not for keeping these things, but rather for not keeping them because of freedom from the law, and newfound liberties in Christ.

"Jesus said to them, 'The Sabbath was made for man, and not man for the Sabbath" (Mark 2:27).

Jesus said the Sabbath was made for man, to provide rest for him, but it really did not and could not. For it was a shadow of things to come- (from Christ). "Come to Me, all who are weary and heavy-laden, and I will give you rest" (Matthew 11:28). "So there remains a Sabbath rest for the people of God" (Hebrews 4:9). Jesus is our rest, and He gives us rest in Him, apart from our works. The early church chose to celebrate this rest on the first day of the week. It is called the Lord's Day because on that day the church celebrates His resurrection.

The Apostle John said, "I was in the Spirit on the Lord's Day, and I heard behind me a loud voice like the sound of a trumpet..." (Revelation 1:10). But this verse does not say the Lord's Day was the first day of the week, so we look elsewhere. "On the first day of the week, when we were gathered together to break bread, Paul began talking to them, intending to leave the next day, and he prolonged his message until midnight" (Acts 20:7). "On the first day of the week each one of you is to put aside and save, as he may prosper, so that no collections be made when I come" (1 Corinthians 16:2). The first day of the week is now when we now gather together, when we assemble ourselves for worship, prayer, fellowship and giving- as His body.

The bottom line is that new believers, Jew, or Gentile, must be born again (John 3:3), of the Spirit and not of the flesh. They must become new creations in Christ. They must let the Old Covenant go. This does not mean to forsake all the godly truths, promises and principles of the Old Testament. It means to have a proper understanding of why it was given. We realize that there were also earlier covenants with Noah and Abraham, and then the law came by Moses. But now we have the law fulfilled and a new and better covenant with Jesus Christ. A good understanding of the Books of Romans, Galatians and Hebrews will best help answering questions regarding these things. All believers, new and old must live their lives for Jesus, by and according to the New Covenant. Above everything else, they are now Christians.

"And He died for all, so that they who live might no longer live for themselves, but for Him who died and rose again on their behalf" (2 Corinthians 5:15).

Let the whole world know – this is the good news.

This is the Gospel.

Jesus said, "Do not think that I came to abolish the Law or the Prophets, I did not come to abolish, <u>but to fulfill</u>" (Matthew 5:17).

<u>Therefore:</u>

"For Christ is the end of the Law for righteousness to everyone who believes" (Romans 10:4).

"It was for freedom that Christ set us free; therefore, keep standing firm and do not be subject again to a yoke of slavery" (Galatians 5:1).

<u>BUT:</u>

"A new commandment I give to you, that you love one another, even as I have loved you, that you also love one another" (John 13:34).

"Bear one another's burdens, and thereby fulfill the law of Christ" (Galatians 6:2).

CHAPTER TWELVE

THE END, - NOW, ALL THINGS BECOME NEW

"Therefore, if anyone is in Christ, he is a new creature; the old things passed away; behold, new things have come" (2 Corinthians 5:17).

JESUS Makes All Things New

One last statement about the fulfillment of Passover is the need to understand that all things have now become new. Judaizers are Jewish Christians who teach it is necessary to adopt old Jewish customs and practices for salvation, especially those found in the Law of Moses. This term is most widely known from its single use in the Greek New Testament (Galatians 2:14). There, Paul publicly challenges Peter for compelling new Gentile converts to Christianity to *Judaize*, that is to be like Jews. It is also known as the Incident at Antioch. The Anchor Bible Dictionary, for example, says: "The clear implication is that the Gentiles are being compelled to live according to Jewish customs."

The early believers were to go into all the world and preach the gospel, making disciples of all nations. They were not to stay in Jerusalem, or any other city, and try to fit in with the old Jewish system at the local synagogues. That would never work now. Jesus said, if they hated Me, they would hate you also. If they persecuted Me, they would persecute you also. For the servant is not greater than the Master. The early church did try to hold on to synagogue involvement, temple worship, and all the Jewish traditions, for that is all they had known. But this was not what God wanted. He was calling out a body of believers from every kindred, tribe, and tongue that would be separated unto Himself. This body of believers would be called the 'church.' Its divine destiny, both individually and collectively, is to become the 'Bride of Christ.'

Jesus also warned His disciples in Matthew 24, Mark 13, and Luke 21, about the up-and-coming destruction of the temple and of the city. The disciples were supposed to leave Jerusalem, for things would never be the same. To leave the temple standing would have allowed things to continue on as they were, with their hypocrisy and their unacceptable sacrifices.

No, it would no longer be, no more temple and no more sacrifices. It is believed that God has allowed the Dome of the Rock to remain on the site of the temple in order that these things would not be reinstituted. Passover is fulfilled. The Apostle Paul warns the church in his letter to the Galatians when he said things like, "Are you so foolish? Having begun by the Spirit, are you now being perfected by the flesh" (Galatians 3:3).

In the Book of Revelation, we read, "And He who sits on the throne said, 'Behold, I am making all things new.' And He said, 'Write, for these words are faithful and true" (Revelation 21:5). We know there will be a new heaven and a new earth; and a new Jerusalem with no more sorrows, nor crying, nor death. All things will be new, but until then He is still making things new spiritually.

To make it perfectly clear the Apostle Paul said, "Therefore if anyone is in Christ, he is a new creature; the old things passed away; behold, new things have come" (2 Corinthians 5:17).

Do you believe this- That all things have become new?

The Fear of Death

"Therefore, since the children share in flesh and blood, He Himself likewise also partook of the same, that through death He might render powerless him who had the power of death, that is, the devil, and might free those who through fear of death were subject to slavery all their lives" (Hebrews 2:14, 15).

No more- All things new! One no longer has to fear death because Jesus has conquered it.

A Need for Sabbath Rest

"For if Joshua had given them rest, He would not have spoken of another day after that. So, there remains a Sabbath rest for the people of God. For the one who has entered His rest has himself also rested from his works, as God did from His. Therefore, let us be diligent to enter that rest, so that no one will fall, through following the same example of disobedience" (Hebrews 4:8-11).

No more- All things new! God's people can finally find rest knowing it is not by works that they are saved, but by His gift of grace through faith. The believer can rest in what Christ has done.

The Need for Priests

"The former priests, on the one hand, existed in greater numbers because they were prevented by death from continuing, but Jesus, on the other hand, because He continues forever, holds His priesthood permanently. Therefore, He is able also to save forever those who draw near to God through Him, since He always lives to make intercession for them" (Hebrews 7:23-25).

No more- All things new! Priests are no longer necessary because we have a great high priest, Jesus Christ, who lives forever and makes intercession for us.

The Need of the Law for Righteousness

"For on the one hand there is a setting aside of a former commandment because of its weakness and uselessness (for the law made nothing perfect)... For if the first covenant had been faultless, there would have been no occasion sought for a second" (Hebrews 7:18, 19 and Hebrews 8:7).

No more- All things new! We have a new commandment which Jesus gave us and a new covenant in His blood. The old laws were unprofitable, weak, and made nothing perfect. His words are now to be written upon our hearts by His Holy Spirit, who leads and guides in all truth. Christ is our righteousness.

The Need for a Holy Temple

"For Christ did NOT enter a holy place made with hands, a mere copy of the true one, but into heaven itself, now to appear in the presence of God for us" (Hebrews 9:24).

No more- All things new! The temple with its lampstands, showbread, the veil, holy of holies, mercy seat, golden sensors and all that which were copies of things in heaven. These are no longer needed nor necessary, for Christ has entered heaven and the presence of God for us as our Great High Priest.

The Need for Offerings and Sacrifices

"Otherwise, would they not have ceased to be offered, because the worshipers, having once been cleansed, would no longer have had consciousness of sins? But in those sacrifices, there is a reminder of sins year by year. For it is impossible for the blood of bulls and goats to take away sins" (Hebrews 10:2-4).

No more- All things new! No longer a need to offer sacrifices. Jesus has appeared to put away sin by the sacrifice of Himself. Christ offered Himself once to bear the sins of many. There is therefore no more sacrifice for sin.

Does the reader see where all this is going? Once Jesus offered Himself as the Passover Lamb, died and rose again- its finished. Now He makes everything new, old things must die. That means the believer needs to let them go.

"So then, you are no longer strangers and aliens, but you are fellow citizens with the saints, and are of God's household, having been built on the foundation of the apostles and prophets, Christ Jesus Himself being the corner stone, in whom the whole building, being fitted together, is growing into a holy temple in the Lord..." (Ephesians 2:19-21).

No temple. There is no longer a need for a temple made by hand- Jesus is the temple in heaven. Now, our bodies become the temple of the Holy Spirit and the kingdom of God is in us.

There is no longer a need for a priesthood- Jesus is our great high priest. The church must quit trying to bring Him down by exalting ourselves as some holier than thou persons.

There are no longer any sacrifices that can be acceptable, for Jesus has offered Himself once for all. Instead, we are to present ourselves as a living sacrifice.

Listen to the Apostle Paul as he fears for the Church

This goes for feast days, months, new moons or any other religious rite or observance.

"Because you are sons, God has sent forth the Spirit of His Son into our hearts, crying, "Abba! Father!" Therefore, you are no longer a slave, but a son, and if a son, then an heir through God. However, at that time, when you did not know God, you were slaves to those which by nature are no gods. But now that you have come to know God, or rather to be known by God, how is it that you turn back again to the weak and worthless elemental things, to which you desire to be enslaved all over again? You observe days and months and seasons and years. I fear for you, that perhaps I have labored over you in vain" (Galatians 4:6-11).

Peter also wants to remind the church

"Knowing that you were not redeemed with perishable things like silver or gold from your futile way of life inherited from your forefathers, but with precious blood, as of a lamb unblemished and spotless, the blood of Christ" (1 Peter 1:18, 19).

The newborn church could not continue in temple worship or synagogue involvement, observances of days, circumcision, etc. for all that was old covenant and is not at all profitable. The new believer should not be concerned with his nationality or ethnicity, no not Jew, Greek nor any Gentile. "There is neither Jew nor Greek, there is neither slave nor free man, there is neither male nor female; for you are all one in Christ Jesus" (Galatians 3:28).

The Church was not to have any walls of separation, doctrines of division, or copies of failed religions or pagan practices. The place of worship was not holy, nor the articles used for worship or fellowship, not the days or seasons to gather, and not even the leaders. Only the believer was to be holy as the Lord is holy. The hour is coming, and now is, when the true worshipers will worship the Father in spirit and truth, for the Father is seeking such to worship Him, Jesus said. God is Spirit, and those who worship him MUST worship in spirit and truth (John 4:21-24).

To the Jew who comes to faith in Jesus Christ and believes He is their Messiah, they must follow the New Testament example and forsake everything else and follow Jesus. Warning: Do not try and make Jesus fit back into your Jewish traditions and heritage, you are now a Christian. You are not a Messianic Jew or anything else. Your heritage is Jewish, but your religion or faith is Christian. Live for Christ and Him alone. "…When a person turns to the Lord, the veil is taken away" (2 Corinthians 3:16).

To the Catholic who comes to faith in Jesus Christ, you too must follow the New Testament example and forsake everything else and follow Jesus. Warning: Do not try and make Jesus fit back into your Catholicism. You have copied the errors of Judaism by imitating all that God has rejected: the priesthood, holy alters, holy water, graven images, sacraments, pennants, calling spiritual men Father, or Holy Father, the worship of Mary, vain repetitious prayers, false doctrines, etc. Let your love of God supersede your love of your religion. Again, "… those who worship him MUST worship in spirit and truth" (John 4:24).

To the Protestant who comes to faith in Jesus Christ, you too must follow the New Testament example and forsake everything and follow Jesus. Warning: Do not try and make Jesus fit back into your Protestant ways. You have the truth, but you do not live the truth. You divide the body of Christ when God has made every effort to unite it and to make it one. You frustrate the grace of God by presuming upon it while you use your liberties to sin and to entertain evil in your life. "For I say to you that unless your righteousness surpasses that of the scribes and Pharisees, you will not enter the kingdom of heaven" (Matthew 5:20).

To the unbeliever, but one who is seeking spiritual truth, and who comes to faith in Jesus Christ, you must follow the New Testament example and forsake everything else and follow Jesus. Warning: Do not settle for religious activity or follow after the traditions of men. Make the Word of God a priority in your life and pray about everything, so that you would be guided by the Holy Spirit. "Let the word of Christ richly dwell within you, with all wisdom teaching and admonishing one another..." (Colossians 3:16).

The believer, as the church, is called out of this world; you are to be different, you are to be separated. You are a peculiar people; you are to be holy as the Lord is holy. Your body is the temple, you are a royal priesthood, you are the saints of God, and your life is to be a living sacrifice.

**** WARNING *****
**** WARNING *****
**** WARNING *****

YOU MUST GET THIS:
OLD THINGS HAVE PASSED AWAY,
ALL THINGS HAVE BECOME NEW.

"But may it never be that I would boast, except in the cross of our Lord Jesus Christ, through which the world has been crucified to me, and I to the world. For neither is circumcision anything, nor uncircumcision, BUT A NEW CREATION" (Galatians 6:14, 15).

New Testament Life

One may be wondering if the early church observed Passover as they did before Christ's death. There is no mention of the church doing so. In fact, the only mention of Passover, outside of the gospels is on two occasions. Once where the Apostle Paul says, "... for Christ, our Passover, also has been sacrificed" (1 Corinthians 5:7).

The context of this verse, both before and afterwards, is the sexual immorality of the church at Corinth. The 'church' is the body of believers that would meet in different houses, such as those at Chloe's (1 Corinthians 1:11). It is the context that is important because the word *festival* is included and must be understood.

"It is actually reported that there is immorality among you, and immorality of such a kind as does not exist even among the Gentiles..." (1 Corinthians 5:1).

"... deliver such a one to Satan for the destruction of the flesh, so that his spirit may be saved in the day of the Lord Jesus" (1 Corinthians 5:5).

These were the actual events going on, and Paul's best advice. "Your boasting is not good. Do you not know that a little leaven leavens the whole lump of dough" (1 Corinthians 5:6)? Although the people knew of the sexual immorality going on, they were boastful about this. Paul addresses this as sin as he likens it to leaven. This was the former reason they were not to have leaven in their house (bread with leaven) for the holy days. This is where Paul goes on to mention Christ as the Passover sacrifice.

"Clean out the old leaven so that you may be a new lump, just as you are in fact unleavened. For Christ our Passover also has been sacrificed. Therefore, let us celebrate the feast, not with the old leaven, nor with the leaven of malice and wickedness, but with the unleavened bread of sincerity and truth. I wrote you in my letter not to associate with immoral people" (1 Corinthians 5:7-9).

Paul's command is to purge out the old leaven, the sin, whether it be out of the camp, out of the church, or out of our individual lives. Why? So, you may be a new lump, and have a new life, without sin, for you truly are 'unleavened.' How so? In that Christ, as our Passover Lamb has been sacrificed for us, for He is the Lamb of God who takes away the sin (leaven) of the world.

Therefore, let us keep the feast- what feast? Not Passover or Unleavened Bread, for that is not the subject here. Just as leaven is sin and being without sin is unleavened, therefore the feast is the celebration of our lives without sin, for it has been dealt with at the cross of Christ. Celebrate our new lives, not with the leaven of malice and wickedness, but with the unleavened bread of sincerity and truth. Amen.

This is not to say that some Jewish feast could not be going on at this time. That is insignificant for that is not what we now celebrate, we are new creations in Christ, for He has made all things new. We truly are unleavened, and we celebrate Jesus and all He has done for us.

The second occasion is Hebrews 11:28.

"By faith Moses, when he had grown up, refused to be called the son of Pharaoh's daughter, choosing rather to endure ill-treatment with the people of God than to enjoy the passing pleasures of sin, considering the reproach of Christ greater riches than the treasures of Egypt: for he was looking to the reward. By faith he left Egypt, not fearing the wrath of the king; for he endured, as seeing Him who is unseen. By faith he kept the Passover and the sprinkling of the blood, so that he who destroyed the firstborn would not touch them" (Hebrews 11:24-28). This one is self-explanatory; in that it reflects back to Moses keeping the Passover by faith and sprinkling the blood on the door posts.

There is one more occasion where the word Passover is used. But it does not appear in the Strong's Exhaustive Concordance[1] as 'Passover.' Twenty-eight times the word 'Passover' appears in the New Testament, and twenty-six times it is in the gospels. The other two times are what has just been covered. Every time the Greek word 'pascha' (Strong's Greek number 3957)[2] is used and translated properly as Passover.

The other occasion, which is the twenty-ninth time, is found in Acts Chapter Twelve. "When he had seized him, he put him in prison, delivering him to four squads of soldiers to guard him, intending after the Passover to bring him out before the people" (Acts 12:4).

The King James Version (KJV), and hence Strong's, translates the Greek word *pascha* in this verse as *Easter* and not as Passover. But as shown, this is the same word translated twenty-eight other times as Passover. Therefore, the word should be Passover and not Easter. The context of this verse is during the week of Passover and the Feast of Unleavened Bread. Knowing they had killed Jesus at this same time of the year, Herod Antipas wanted to clamp down on the believers to please the Jews, again.

"Now about that time Herod the king laid hands on some who belonged to the church in order to mistreat them. And he had James the brother of John put to death with a sword. When he saw that it pleased the Jews, he proceeded to arrest Peter also. Now it was during the days of Unleavened Bread. When he had seized him, he put him in prison, delivering him to four squads of soldiers to guard him, intending after the Passover to bring him out before the people. So, Peter was kept in the prison, but prayer for him was being made fervently by the church to God" (Acts 12:1-5).

The Book of Acts covers the period up until Paul's imprisonment at Rome in 61 A.D. Herod Antipas, the Tetrarch, whom John the Baptist rebuked, died in 39 A.D. (Luke 3:19). Therefore, this event in Acts Twelve is only a few years after Jesus' death in 34 A.D. This time of the year certainly was during the time of His resurrection and the church may have well been celebrating it as such. But there is no Biblical account or reference to anything as officially observed at this time, and there was no command to do so. The context does not support the use of the word 'Easter' here in this text. This is about Herod and the Jews and their persecution of James and Peter. They were to hold Peter in prison until after the 'Passover.' This is eerily similar to them wanting to seize and kill Jesus after the Passover (Matthew 26:3-5).

It is 'Easter' in the King James Version, published in 1611, and it may be by that time in 'church history' such observances may have begun to be commemorated. Be it known though that the same Greek, and Latin, word *pascha* that was being translated as Passover, is now being translated as *Easter.* Easter is the celebration of Christ's resurrection, which followed both His death on the cross and the three days and three nights of His burial.

IN CONCLUSION

Passover is fulfilled; therefore, the believer does not celebrate Passover; the believer (Jew or Gentile) celebrates Jesus and the redemption He alone has supplied for them. All that the Law required Jesus has fulfilled; and He now makes all things new. Jesus gave His church a new commandment to live by, with a new and better covenant. The believer is to walk in newness of life as they look forward to the New Jerusalem.

Listen to these witnesses.

The Angel said (looking forward in time), "...And you shall call His name Jesus, for He shall save His people from their sins" (Matthew 1:21).

Job said (looking forward in time), "Yet as for me, I know that my Redeemer lives and at the last He will take His stand on the earth" (Job 19:25).

John the Baptist said (in the present time), "Behold the Lamb of God who takes away the sin of the world" (John 1:29).

Paul the Apostle said (looking back in time), "For Christ our Passover also has been sacrificed" (1 Corinthians 5:7b). "For Christ is the end of the law for righteousness to everyone who believes" (Romans 10:4).

The Gospel of Jesus Christ has caused many to be offended and turn away, while it yet continues to draw myriads of followers over the centuries. The Scriptures declare: "I am not ashamed of the gospel for it is the power of God for salvation to everyone who believes..." (Romans 1:16).

The Epistle to the Hebrews stands in its entirety as our final witness to the truths mentioned in this study. "For this reason, we must pay much closer attention to what we have heard, so we do not drift away..." (Hebrews 2:1). (Please take time to read this Epistle to the Hebrews.)

NOW:

Seeing how we are surrounded with so great a cloud of witnesses; please let what Jesus did on the cross, as the Passover Lamb of God, redeem you from your sins! Tell Him that you turn your life over to Him and that you will follow His word and His will for your life. Become His disciple and learn of Him, for His burden is easy, and His yoke is light. No longer live for yourself but for Him who died for you and rose again. By grace you can be saved through faith, it is the gift of God. Understand that the wages of sin is death, but the gift of God is eternal life through Christ our Lord. We cannot save ourselves; Jesus is the Savior.

Jesus said we cannot be His disciples unless we love Him more than anything else, unless we bear our cross and follow Him, unless we first count the cost and then finish the course, and unless we are willing to forsake all for His sake (Luke 14:25-32). All must be born again and become a new creation in Christ as Christians in order that we may be His disciples. We Must!

Like the prodigal son (Luke 15:11-32) we all must acknowledge the sin that we are in (for all have sinned (Romans 3:23). We must have a change of heart and mind concerning our personal offense against our heavenly Father. With honest and sincere words and actions (an act of surrender), we determine with our minds that we are not going to live this way any longer (an act of repentance). And with our hearts we place our full trust in Jesus Christ to save us by grace through His finished work on the cross (an act of faith). The evidence of that sincerity will be a changed life through the now indwelling of the Holy Spirit who has heard and honored our prayers. Returning to our Father means we now will live for Him whom He sent to die for us. This He did while we were still in our trespasses and sins (Romans 5:8). May we all return to our Father's house, He is waiting with open arms (Luke 15:20).

"It was for freedom that Christ set us free; therefore, keep standing firm and do not be subject again to a yoke of slavery" (Galatians 5:1).

Let us wrap this up as it now calls for your decision.

CHAPTER THIRTEEN

SUMMARY
(OR CLOSING SUMMATION)

A Brief Summary of the Findings

The Supper Meal

1. On Nisan 14, the fifth day of the Jewish week, (our Thursday) Jesus ate an evening meal which is call the Lord's Supper, at the beginning of the day of Passover. Remember that the Jewish day began at evening time. The disciple's intent was to find a 'place' to prepare for Passover. Although the lambs for the Passover meal were not killed until around 3 p.m. the following afternoon, this supper meal focused on the bread and the wine. The old customs were passing, and things were becoming new.

    This is the meal where communion was instituted as Paul quotes Jesus as saying, the bread is His body, and the cup is His blood of the new covenant. "Do this in remembrance of Me," Jesus said. This will be the end of the Old Covenant and the beginning of the New. The meal would no longer be one of the yearly Passover's remembrance on a particular day of the year. Now it would be to declare the Lord's death, the shedding His blood and the giving of His body for our redemption, until He comes again. No matter how often it is done, it is done in remembrance of Jesus, the Lamb of God, sacrificed for us.

The Garden, The Betrayal, The Crucifixion

2. After dinner they went to the garden of Gethsemane and spent some time there. This is when Jesus prays to be able to make it to the cross despite how He is feeling and thinking. Here is where Judas Iscariot betrays Jesus with a kiss. The guards later take Him to Caiaphas and then to Pilate in the early morning hours. Finding no fault in Him, but wanting to please the people, Jesus was ordered to be crucified. At 9 a.m. He was nailed to the cross and at 3 p.m., when the lambs would be killed, Jesus died as our Passover Lamb. It was approximately three hours before the following day that would begin at 6 p.m.

The Burial, in the Tomb, the 1st Day

3. Therefore, Jesus needed to be removed from the cross and be placed in a tomb as soon as possible, for none of that could be done on a Sabbath Day. The next day, coming at evening time, would be Nisan 15, the sixth day of the Jewish week (our Friday). This would be the first day of the Feast of Unleavened Bread, which is a High Sabbath Day. Joseph of Arimathea asked for the body of Jesus, before evening time, and placed Jesus in his tomb. It was still the fifth day of the week, Nisan 14, our Thursday. The Jewish leaders set a guard because He said He would rise in three days.

THE SIGN OF JONAH

> *"For just as Jonah was three days and three nights in the belly of the sea monster, so will the Son of Man will be three days and three nights in the heart of the earth" (Matthew 12:40).*

According to the sign of Jonah this Thursday afternoon would be the first day in the heart of the earth. If Jesus said He would rise the same day this would be it, but He did not. He said in three days.

The 1ˢᵗ Night & 2ⁿᵈ Day, the High Sabbath

4. On Nisan 15, the sixth day of the Jewish week (our Friday) which began at evening time, it was a High Sabbath. It was now the first night that Jesus was in the tomb and of the sign of Jonah. It being a High Sabbath, no work could be done in the daylight hours to follow. The evening hours, during the dark, was the first night; but then during the daylight hours of the same day, it would now be the second day of the sign of Jonah. If Jesus said He would rise in one day this would be it, but He did not. He said He would rise in three days, so this is only one day so far toward that.

The 2ⁿᵈ Night and 3ʳᵈ Day, the weekly Sabbath

5. On Nisan 16, the seventh day of the Jewish week (our Saturday), it is the regular weekly Sabbath. There are back-to-back Sabbaths this year because of Passover falling on the fifth day of the week (our Thursday). Again, remember the day begins at evening time, so this is now the second night of the sign of Jonah. During the upcoming daylight hours, it would be the third day of the sign of Jonah. Being

a Sabbath, no work was done, and so no one went to the tomb because they could not do anything anyway. Also, the guards were posted, and the stone had been rolled in front of the opening. If Jesus said He would rise in two days this would be it, but He did not. He said in three days, so this is only the second day so far.

The 3rd Night, and The Resurrection Before Dawn

6. On Nisan 17, the first day of the Jewish week (our Sunday) which began in the evening hours, the Sabbath was over, but it was dark, and no one went out to do anything except thieves and robbers. This was the third night of the sign of Jonah that Jesus had told us about. Now we know that the women went to the tomb toward the dawn of day, and the time does not really matter, because HE WAS ALREADY RISEN when they got there, no matter when it was. The important thing is that He rose during the third night and before the fourth day, which the daylight hours of the first day of the Jewish week (our Sunday) would have been. All four gospels agree that it was the first day of the Jewish week and that He had already risen. Jesus rose on our Sunday morning during the darkness of the morning hours. Jesus said He would rise in three days and this is now that third day, and truly, truly... HE IS RISEN INDEED.

The Years of John and Jesus' Ministries

7. It is known from the years of the reign of Tiberius Caesar, that the year John the Baptist began his ministry was 29 A.D. From that it can be determined that Jesus began His ministry sometime afterward in 30 A.D., being about 30 years of age. A minimum of three Passovers, after His ministry began,

are recorded before His death. This brings it to at least 32 A.D. or even 34 A.D. Knowing the years of the reign of Biblical figures, especially Pontius Pilate and Caiaphas give a good range of years. One can know with a high degree of certainty the years in which there needs to be a Passover that fell on the Jewish fifth day (our Thursday) to prove the presuppositions that it was between 32 A.D. and 36 A.D.

The Back-to-Back Sabbath Findings

8. Being able to show the back-to-back Sabbaths is the real clincher here, which some people either have no idea of, will not consider, or they completely dismiss it. Not us, we want the truth.

The U.S. Naval Observatory Findings

9. The U.S. Naval Observatory Astronomical Applications Department confirms our findings with an April 22, 34 A.D. Passover on a Thursday. This plus the ability to show how the two calendars, the Hebrew, and the Julian, cannot be looked at side by side because they do not consider the fact that 3/4th of the time they are the exact same day. A look at the other surrounding years of 31 A.D. to 36 A.D. do not fit the criteria either for a fifth day of the week Passover.

    All the extra data[1] provided displays their accuracy in this matter.

Jesus' Fulfillment of Old Testament Law and Types

10. Jesus did fulfill all that the Law of the Lord required relating to the Passover Lamb. All that was concealed in the Old Testament laws and requirements, even the types and

shadows, have fully been revealed and fulfilled in the New Testament in the person of Jesus Christ.

A. Jesus was the firstborn Son.
B. He was sacrificed at Jerusalem
C. He was chosen on the 10th of Nisan by the people (by their Hosanna's).
D. He was without blemish (sinless).
E. He was taken outside the gates to be killed.
F. His bones were not broken.
G. His flesh was the unleavened bread (without sin).
H. His blood was shed upon the two pieces of wood.
I. His blood was the blood of the New Covenant
J. He, as the Passover Lamb, was killed on Nisan 14 at twilight.
K. He has been given authority to execute judgment.
L. His blood causes the believer to be passed over from death, to life.
M. We remember till He comes again, He shed His blood and gave His life to redeem us from sin, and to give us eternal life.

The importance of it all cannot be overstated and must be understood by the believer. The ransom for our lives was paid by the life that Jesus gave and the blood that He shed. Jesus destroyed the works and the power of the devil over us, having nailed to the cross all our sins and transgressions that were against us. Our Lord has supplied abundant life for us through His death, resurrection, and the coming of the Holy Spirit that enables us to live victoriously.

Our great redemption by the Lamb of God is a finished work.

Passover is just that now– over. The Law has been fulfilled. All that pointed to Jesus, the feasts, the priesthood, the sin offerings, the sacrificial lamb, and the signs, symbols and shadows, were all intended for us not to miss His initial coming. Now, and until Jesus comes again, we declare His gospel and the finished work that He carried out. Next, we see Jesus continuing into eternity as the Lamb Himself, and He is the only one who is to be worshipped and adored by all of God's created beings.

The Law and Prophets have been Fulfilled

11. The church today must, as the early church had to, let go of the first (old) covenant because a new and better has come. Jesus was preparing His disciples and followers for the time when the first covenant (the law and religious traditions) would cease. It would not just end but it would be fulfilled. Because Jesus said that He did not come to destroy the law, this meant that with the coming of the Holy Spirit, the spirit of the law is still to be pertinent. This is where Jesus said, *'But I say,'* that is the part we must adhere to, or, that which is rightfully required. This is saying that we should not only not murder, but we should not hate. And not only should we not hate, but we should love. And not only should we love, but we should also forgive and bless our enemy and those who despise us. This is the spirit of the law and new covenant. It is not avoiding wrongdoing but doing what is right for the glory of our Father in heaven.

Jesus Makes All Things New

12. Now the early church struggled with this new message. They struggled because of the ever-present dangers of religion itself, and because of the revised call for the just to live by faith. They had to realize the old covenant was over and that a new covenant had come. We realized this by the many

excerpts from the Book of Hebrews showing the end of all major ceremonial demands of the law. It was the unbelieving Jews that came after Paul, just as they did Jesus, to silence his message. There are other books of the Bible that show how the new Jewish converts struggled with letting go of the Old Covenant to the point they were called Judaizers. This meant they were trying to get new believers to hold to the Old Covenant, which includes the works of the law, such as circumcision, as a part of their salvation.

The bottom line is that new believers, **Jew or Gentile**, great or small, male or female, white or black, American or Arab, rich or poor, slave or free, hurt or healed, all must be born again of the Spirit, and not of the flesh (John 3:3). This includes becoming new creations in Christ, for it is written; "Therefore if anyone is in Christ, old things are passed away; behold, all things are become new" (2 Corinthians 5:17).

That is it, ALL THINGS must become new! What then, or who then, am I now? Read on....

I

AM

A

NEW

CREATION

IN

CHRIST JESUS

"And He said to him, "You shall love the Lord your God with all your heart, and with all your soul, and with all your mind." This is the great and foremost commandment. The second is like it, "You shall love your neighbor as yourself." On these two commandments depend the whole Law and the Prophets" (Matthew 22:37-40).

REFERENCES

Scripture

All Scriptures are from the New American Standard Bible.

Since its completion in 1971, the New American Standard Bible has been widely embraced as a literal and accurate English translation because it consistently uses the formal equivalence translation philosophy. This method translates word-for-word from the original languages as much as possible. At the same time, it recognizes the need for the translation to be readable. Millions of people have trusted the NASB for connecting with God while reading, learning, and applying the Bible's teaching and wisdom to the demands of daily life. The accuracy of the NASB makes it a trusted choice of many students, scholars, pastors, and missionaries as they study and teach the Word of God. Read the NASB for yourself and discover the original meaning of the biblical texts. (Lockman.org)

Calendars

All calendars were computer generated.

Introduction

I-1. Good Friday

It is the Friday before Easter, the day on which Christians annually observe the commemoration of the Crucifixion of Jesus Christ. From the early days of Christianity, Good Friday was observed as a day of sorrow, penance, and <u>fasting</u>, a characteristic that finds expression in the German word *Karfreitag* -"Sorrowful Friday." (Brittannica.com)

I-2. Jerusalem 70 A.D.

The Roman military blockade of Jerusalem occurred during the First Jewish Revolt (70 CE). The Romans destroyed much of the city, including the Second Temple. The majority of information on the siege comes from the copious notes of the Jewish historian Flavius Josephus. (Brittannica.com)

Chapter One

1-1. Tekufah

(lit. "turn," "cycle"): <u>Seasons.</u>

Seasons of the year. The four tekufot are: (1) Tekufat Nisan, the vernal equinox (March 21), when the sun enters Aries; this is the beginning of spring, or "'et hazera'" (seed-time), when day and night are equal; (2) Tekufat Tammuz, the summer solstice (June 21), when the sun enters Cancer; this is the summer season, or "'et ha-kazir" (harvest-time), when the day is the longest in the year; (3) Tekufat Tishri, the autumnal equinox (Sept. 23), when the sun enters Libra, and autumn, or "'et ha-hazir" (vintage-time), begins, and when the day again equals the night; (4) Tekufat Tebet, the winter solstice (Dec. 22), when the sun enters Capricornus; this is the beginning of winter, or "'et ha-horef"(stripping-time), when the night is the longest during the year. Each tekufah, according to Samuel Yarhinai, marks the beginning of a period of 91 days and 7½ hours. (Jewishencyclopedia.com)

1-2. Equinox

Equinox descends from aequus, the Latin word for "equal," and nox, the Latin word for "night"—a fitting history for a word that describes days of the year when the daytime and nighttime are equal in length.

In the northern hemisphere, the vernal equinox marks the first day of spring and occurs when the sun moves north across the equator. (Vernal comes from the Latin word ver, meaning "spring.") The autumnal equinox marks the first day of autumn in the northern hemisphere and occurs when the sun crosses the equator going south. In contrast, a solstice is either of the two moments in the year when the sun's apparent path is farthest north or south from the equator. (Merriam-Webster.com)

1-3. Days in Hebrew Months
The Months of the Jewish Calendar. Ever since G-d took us out of Egypt, the Jewish people have been keeping track of time—and celebrating the festivals—according to the lunar calendar, which contains 12 (or 13) months. Every month is either 29 or 30 days long, beginning (and ending) on a special day known as Rosh Chodesh ("The Head of the Month"). The months were once declared by a beit din (rabbinical court) after the new moon had been sighted, but now follow a predetermined calendar. (Chabad.org)

1-4. Passover
"Speak to all the congregation of Israel, saying, 'On the tenth of this month they are, each one, to take a lamb for themselves, according to the fathers' households, a lamb for each household. Your lamb shall be an unblemished male a year old; you may take it from the sheep or from the goats. You shall keep it until the fourteenth day of the same month, then the whole assembly of the congregation of Israel is to slaughter it at twilight. Moreover, they shall take some of the blood and put it on the two doorposts and on the lintel of the houses in which they eat it. —it is the LORD's Passover. The blood shall be a sign for you on the houses where you live; and when I see the blood I will pass over you..." (Exodus 12:3-13). (Biblegateway.com)

1-5. Abib

Pronounced \ ä-'vēv \ Definition of Abib: the first month of the ancient Hebrew calendar corresponding to Nisan. (Merriam-Webster.com)

1-6. Nisan

In the ancient Hebrew calendar: the first month of the ecclesiastical year and the seventh of the civil year, corresponding to the latter part of March and the early part of April. Later called by the Babylonian name Nisan. (Lexico.com)

1-7. Ahasuerus

Ahasuerus, the Persian king of the Book of Esther, being identified by the rabbis with the one mentioned in Dan. ix. 1 as father of Darius, king of Media, and with the one mentioned in Ezra, iv. 6, is counted as one of the three kings of Biblical history who ruled over the entire globe, the other two being Ahab and Nebuchadnezzar. Persian king, identical with Xerxes (486-465 B.C.). The Book of Esther deals only with one period of his reign. (Jewishencyclopedia.com)

1-8. Babylonian Exile

Era: 70 years of Babylonian Empire (analysis of Jeremiah's time prophecy) Dates: 3615 - 3685 AM, 609 - 539 B.C. Biblical Chapter References: 2 Chronicles 36, Jeremiah 25, 29; Daniel 1, 9. This is what the Lord says: "When seventy years are completed for Babylon, I will come to you and fulfill my gracious promise to bring you back to this place." Jeremiah 29:10 (NIV). (Bibleworldhistory.com)

1-9. Passion Week

Holy Week, in the Christian church, the week between Palm Sunday and Easter, observed with special solemnity as a time of devotion to the Passion of Jesus Christ. In the Greek and Roman liturgical books, it is called the Great Week because great deeds were done by God during this week. The name Holy Week was used in the 4th century by St. Athanasius, bishop of Alexandria, and St. Epiphanius of Constantia. Originally, only Good Friday and Holy Saturday were observed as holy days. Later, Wednesday was added as the day on which Judas plotted to betray Jesus, and by the beginning of the 3rd century the other days of the week had been added. The pre-Nicene church concentrated its attention on the celebration of one great feast, the Christian Passover, on the night between Saturday and Easter Sunday morning. By the later 4th century the practice had begun of separating the various events and <u>commemorating</u> them on the days of the week on which they occurred: Judas's betrayal and the institution of the Eucharist on Maundy Thursday; the Passion and death of Christ on Good Friday; his burial on Saturday; and his Resurrection on Easter Sunday. (Brittannica.com)

Chapter Two

2-1. The Year 3795

The Dating of the Hebrew Calendar Year. Israel's official calendar is the Hebrew one. Under law, official Israeli documents must have the Hebrew date on them. Moreover, holidays in Israel are determined according to the Jewish calendar, not the Gregorian one. That is because the Gregorian and the Jewish calendars do not coincide. The Hebrew calendar is very complicated, because it has to align the solar year (365 days, 5 hours, 48 minutes and 46-seconds) with the lunar year (12 months of 29 days, 12 hours, 44 minutes and 3 seconds). October 7, 3761 B.C.E., is the date on which the world was created – according to the Hebrew calendar that governs the passage of time among the Jewish people. The calculation of the year is fairly simple to understand; how the precise day and month were arrived at is a little more complicated. "According to the Hebrew calendar, the year just begun *(in 2015)* is 5776. If we subtract 2015 – the current year in the secular, or Gregorian, calendar – from that,

we arrive at Year One being 3761 B.C.E. (Before the Common Era)."
(Haaretz.com)

[The year 3761 (Year One) plus 34 (A.D.) equals the year 3795 on the Hebrew Calendar for the year in which Jesus was crucified.]

2-2. Passion Week
– same reference as 1.9

2-3. United States Naval Observatory Astronomical Applications Department

Passover dates 26-34 A.D. The following astronomical data in the first three columns were obtained from the U.S. Naval Observatory Astronomical Applications Department. The pertinent file may be accessed on the Internet at: http://aa.usno.navy.mil/data/docs/SpringPhenom.html.

Chapter Three

3-1. Josephus

Flavius Josephus (37 – 100 CE) (a.k.a. Joseph ben Matityahu in Hebrew) was a Jew who grew up in Jerusalem at the beginning of the Common Era. He was well educated, knowing both Jewish texts and the Greek language (although his Greek grammar was faulty). During the Great Revolt from 66-73 CE, Josephus served as a general of the Galilee. Josephus' second major work, Jewish Antiquities, described the entire history of the Jews. It included a great deal of material from the time of Alexander the Great to the destruction of the Second Temple. However, because of Josephus' proclivity to depend on hearsay and legend, scholars are never sure what to accept as fact. (Jewishvirtuallibrary.org)

3-2. Communion

capitalized: A Christian <u>sacrament</u> in which <u>consecrated</u> bread and wine are consumed as memorials of Christ's death or as symbols for the realization of a spiritual union between Christ and communicant or as the body and blood of Christ. (Merriam-Webster.com)

3-3. New Covenant

The Book of Hebrews is a declaration of the absolute supremacy of Jesus Christ. Hebrews tells us that Jesus is superior to the angels (Chapters 1–2), superior to Moses (3–4:13), and superior to Aaron (4:14–7). His is a superior priesthood (8–10:18), and He has inaugurated a superior covenant (10:19–13). Throughout the book of Hebrews, we find this emphasis on that which is new and better. (Ligonier.org)

3-4. Old Covenant

What were the limitations of the old covenant? The writer of Hebrews talked about that in 10:1-4. First of all, the old covenant was a shadow and not the substance. Hebrews 10:1 says, "For the Law, since it has only a shadow of the good things to come and not the very form of things, can never, by the same sacrifices which they offer continually year by year, make perfect those who draw near." The writer said the Law was "not the very form of things." The Greek word for "form" is "eikon." An icon is a perfect representation of something else. That is what the Law was. There were Christians in Paul's day who wanted to go back under the dietary restrictions of the Old Testament. They wanted to go back under the Sabbath restrictions. They wanted to celebrate all the Jewish holidays. And Paul, who was a Hebrew of the Hebrews, was saying, "Forget all that stuff. That is old, that is ancient, and it is a shadow of something better yet to come–Jesus. Those things are the shadow. Jesus is the substance." (ptv.org)

Chapter Four

4-1. Hematohidrosis

A rare clinical phenomenon in the Indian Journal of Dermatology 2009 Jul-Sep; 54 (3): 290–292. doi: [10.4103/0019-5154.55645] PMCID: PMC2810702, PMID: 20161867

Hematohidrosis is a rare clinical condition of sweating blood. It may occur when a person is suffering from extreme stress, for example, facing his or her own death. (Indian Dermatology Online Journal) Hematidrosis, author. [Last cited on 4 July 2010]. (ncbi.nlm.nih.gov)

Chapter Five

5-1. Abraham's Bosom

"Now the poor man died and was carried away by the angels to Abraham's bosom; and the rich man also died and was buried. In Hades he lifted up his eyes, being in torment, and saw Abraham far away and Lazarus in his bosom. And he cried out and said, 'Father Abraham, have mercy on me, and send Lazarus so that he may dip the tip of his finger in water and cool off my tongue, for I am in agony in this flame.' But Abraham said, 'Child, remember that during your life you received your good things, and likewise Lazarus bad things; but now he is being comforted here, and you are in agony. And besides all this, between us and you there is a great chasm fixed, so that those who wish to come over from here to you will not be able, and *that* none may cross over from there to us" (Luke 16:22-26). (Biblegateway.com)

5-2. Synagogue

When the institution of the synagogue began to emerge, the Temple in Jerusalem was still standing. The first roles of the synagogue were not associated with prayer, but rather with Jewish study and gathering. The first rabbis were not celebrants of religious rites but teachers of religious texts; in fact, the word rabbi means "my teacher." Following the destruction of the Temple in 70 CE, the synagogue assumed an additional role as the place of communal prayer. No distinct architectural forms for synagogue buildings became standard, but the interior design came to include features still found today: a lectern for the leader of the service, a "Holy Ark" in which Torah scrolls are kept, and seating arranged facing Jerusalem, in honor of the centrality of the site of the former Temple. (myjewishlearning.com)

5-3. Jewish Days of the Week

With the exception of the Shabbat, the weekdays are simply numbered 1 - 6.

1. Yom rishon = "first day" = (Sunday)
2. Yom sheni = "second day" = (Monday)
3. Yom sh'lishi = "third day" = (Tuesday)
4. Yom revi'l = "fourth day" = (Wednesday)
5. Yom chamishi = "fifth day" = (Thursday)
6. Yom shishi = "sixth day" = (Friday)
7. The week culminates on the "seventh day", the Holy Shabbat (Shabbat kodesh) (Jewishgen.org)

5-4. First Fruits

First Fruits, that portion of the fruits of each year's harvest that following the biblical injunction was to be taken to the Temple in Jerusalem. In the Bible: The Hebrew term bikkurim and related terms for the "first fruits" derive from the same root as bekhor, "firstborn (see *Firstborn). On the same general principle that the firstborn of man and beast belonged to the God of Israel and were to be devoted to Him, the first fruits, including the first grains to ripen each season, were to be brought as an offering to God. Every Israelite who possessed the means of agricultural productivity was under this obligation (Exodus 23:19; 34:26; Numbers 15:17–21; 18:12–3; Deuteronomy 26:1-11). (Jewishvirtuallibrary.org)

5-5. Feast of Pentecost

The Feast of the Fiftieth Day has been a many-sided one (comp. Book of Jubilees, vi. 21: "This feast is twofold and of a double nature"), and as a consequence has been called by many names. In the Old Testament it is called the "Feast of Harvest" ("Ḥag ha-Ḳaẓir"; Ex. xxiii. 16) and the "Feast of Weeks" ("Ḥag Shabu'ot"; *ib.* xxxiv. 22; Deut. xvi. 10; II Chron. viii. 13; Aramaic, "Ḥagga di-Shebu'aya," Men. 65a; Greek, ἑορτὴ ἑβδομάδων), also the "Day of the First-Fruits" ("Yom ha-Bikkurim"; Num. xxviii. 26; (Jewishencyclopedia.com)

5-6. Putrefaction

The Stages of Human Decomposition: Human decomposition is a natural process involving the breakdown of tissues after death. While the rate of human decomposition varies due to several factors, including weather, temperature, moisture, pH and oxygen levels, cause of death, and body position, all human bodies follow the same four stages of human decomposition. Stage One: Autolysis, Stage Two: Bloat (includes putrefaction), Stage Three: Active decay, and Stage Four: Skeletonization. (Aftermath.com)

Chapter Seven

7-1. Historical Figures

Pontius Pilate was the fifth procurator, appointed in 26 A.D., condemned Jesus to death in 30 A.D. (see Matthew 27:11-26). **Philip (Herod Philip II)** ruled as tetrarch of **Ituraea** and **Trachonitis** to the north east of the **Sea of Galilee** from 4 B.C. to 34 A.D. (see Luke 3:1). **Herod Agrippa** executed the apostle James (the brother of John), and arrested Peter, who had a miraculous escape (see Acts 12:1-19). Herod Agrippa I, died in 39 A.D.) **Tiberius**, in full Tiberius

Caesar Augustus or Tiberius Julius Caesar Augustus, original name Tiberius Claudius Nero, (born November 16, 42 BCE—died March 16, 37 CE, Capreae [Capri], near Naples), second Roman emperor (14–37 CE). (Britannica.com) Herod the great died between 4 B.C. and 1 B.C. by many sources. **Lysanias** The reference to Lysanias in Luke 3:1 as the tetrarch of Abilene NW of Damascus may be a mistake, since the only Lysanias certainly known died in 36 BCE. There was, however, possibly another, unknown, Lysanias in the fifteenth year of the reign of Tiberius (28 or 29 CE) to which Luke is referring, since an inscription bearing the name Lysanias was found at Abila, the city in Abilene, and dated between 14 and 29 CE. (Oxfordbiblicalstudies.com)

7-2. Kings

Nebuchadnezzar II	King of Babylon 605-561 reign
Nabonidus	King of Babylon 556-539
Belshazzar	King of Babylon till death in 539
Cyrus II	King of Persia 539-529
Darius I	King of Persia 522-486
Xerxes	King of Persia 485-464
Artaxerxes I	King of Persia 465-424
Darius II	King of Persia 423-404
Artaxerxes II	King of Persia 404-358
Artaxerxes III	King of Persia 358-338

Reign of Kings, years are B.C. (Encyclopedia Britannica)

7-3. Metonic Cycle

Metonic cycle, in chronology, a period of 19 years in which there are 235 lunations, or synodic months, after which the Moon's phases recur on the same days of the solar year, or year of the seasons. The cycle was discovered by Meton (fl. 432 BC), an Athenian astronomer. Computation from modern data shows that 235 lunations are 6,939 days, 16.5 hours: and 19 solar years, 6,939 days, 14.5 hours. (Britannica.com)

7-4. Jewish Calendar

Month	Length	Gregorian Equivalent
Nissan	30 days	March-April
Iyar	29 days	April-May
Sivan	30 days	May-June
Tammuz	29 days	June-July
Av	30 days	July-August
Elul	29 days	August-September
Tishri	30 days	September-October
Heshvan	29 or 30 days	October-November
Kislev	30 or 29 days	November-December
Tevet	29 days	December-January
Shevat	30 days	January-February
Adar*	29 or 30 days	February-March

*In non-leap years Adar has 29 days.

*In leap years Adar has 30 days.

(Jewishvirtuallibrary.org)

7.4 Jewish Calendar

7-5. Fig Tree
Symbolic of Israel in Scripture: Hosea 9:10; Jerimiah 24:3-10 and Jeremiah 29:16, 17.

7-6. Jerusalem 70 A.D.
Siege of Jerusalem, (70 CE), Roman military blockade Jerusalem during the First Jewish Revolt. The fall of the city marked the effective conclusion of a four-year campaign against the Jewish insurgency in Judaea. The Romans destroyed much of the city, including the Second Temple. The majority of information on the siege comes from the copious notes of the Jewish historian Flavius Josephus. (Britannica.com)

Chapter Eight

8-1. United States Naval Observatory Applications Department
Topics include:

Calendars and Historical Events
Converting Between Julian Dates and Gregorian Calendar Dates
Universal Time and Greenwich Mean Time
Length of Day and Night at the Equinoxes
Visibility of the Crescent Moon
Length of Day and Night at the Equinoxes
Introduction to Calendars
Spring Phenomena, 25 BCE to 38 CE
(usno.navy.mil)

8-2. USNOAD Findings
The complete findings for Passover dates from 26 A.D. to 34 A.D. from their website, http://aa.usno.navy.mil/data/docs/SpringPhenom.html, were recorded on the Intercontinental Church of God website. (Intercontinentalcog.org)

8-3. Figure 2
The results of the findings of the USNOAD Passover dates 26-34 A.D. are given in this Figure from information here. intercontinentalcog.org › Appendix › Passover_dates_2...
Passover dates 26-34 A.D. The following astronomical data in the first three columns below were obtained from the U.S. Naval Observatory Astronomical ...
(intercontinentalcog.org/Appendix/Passover_dates_26-34_AD.php)

8-4. Julian and Gregorian Calendars
The Julian calendar was introduced by Julius Caesar in 46 B.C. It's believed that it was created by Egyptian astronomers (Alexandrian astronomers headed by Sozigen) although named after Julius. It

acquired it's final form in 8 A.D. The year started from the 1ˢᵗ of January because in that day the elected consuls entered the post and then there was 12 months, 365 or sometimes 366 days. And that "sometimes" differentiate it from the Gregorian calendar *(1582)*. Finally, Pope Gregory XIII reformed the calendar and made what is known as Gregorian calendar. This project was carried out by Luigi Lilio, and according to him, later we should consider leap years only those century years that can be divided by 4 without residue (1600, 2000, 2400) and other should be considered as regular. Also, the deviation of 10 days that accumulated since 8 A.D. was eliminated and according to pope's decree from 24 February 1582, after 4ᵗʰ of October 1582 the 15ᵗʰ of October should follow. (Britannica.com)

8-5. Year 3795
– Same as 2.1, (cgsf.org)

Chapter Ten

11-1. Judaizer
Word forms: 'Juda,ized' or 'Juda,izing'

    a. To conform to Jewish morality, traditions, etc. Verb Transitive
    b. To bring into conformity with Judaism. (collinsdictionary.com)

Chapter Twelve

12-1. Strong's Exhaustive Concordance
The Strong's Exhaustive Concordance is the most complete, easy-to-use, and understandable concordance for studying the original languages of the Bible. Combining the text of the King James Version and New American Standard Bibles with the power of the Greek and

Hebrew Lexicons, any student or pastor can gain a clear understanding of the Word to enrich their study. (Biblestudytools.com)

12-2 Strong's Greek number 3957

Strong's Concordance 3957. pascha

pascha: the Passover, the Passover supper or lamb

Original Word: πάσχα, τό

Part of Speech: Aramaic Transliterated Word (Indeclinable)

Transliteration: pascha

Phonetic Spelling: (pas'-khah)

Definition: the Passover, the Passover supper or lamb

Usage: the feast of Passover, the Passover lamb.

(Biblehub.com)

Chapter Thirteen

13-1. Extra Tables

FIRST TABLE
VERNAL EQUINOX

Julian		Greenwich		Julian		Greenwich	
Calendar	Date	Time	Week Day	Calendar	Date	Time	Week Day
BCE	March			CE	March		
25	22	8 p.m.	Saturday	7	23	8 a.m.	Wednesday
24	23	2 a.m.	Monday	8	22	2 p.m.	Thursday
23	23	8 a.m.	Tuesday	9	22	8 p.m.	Friday
22	23	1 p.m.	Wednesday	10	23	1 a.m.	Sunday
21	22	7 p.m.	Thursday	11	23	7 a.m.	Monday
20	23	1 a.m.	Saturday	12	22	1 p.m.	Tuesday
19	23	7 a.m.	Sunday	13	22	7 p.m.	Wednesday
18	23	1 p.m.	Monday	14	23	1 a.m.	Friday
17	22	6 p.m.	Tuesday	15	23	7 a.m.	Saturday
16	23	0*	Thursday	16	22	Noon	Sunday
15	23	6 a.m.	Friday	17	22	6 p.m.	Monday

14	23	Noon	Saturday	18	23	0*	Wednesday
13	22	6 p.m.	Sunday	19	23	6 a.m.	Thursday
12	22	11 p.m.	Monday	20	22	Noon	Friday
11	23	5 a.m.	Wednesday	21	22	6 p.m.	Saturday
10	23	11 a.m.	Thursday	22	22	11 p.m.	Sunday
9	22	5 p.m.	Friday	23	23	5 a.m.	Tuesday
8	22	11 p.m.	Saturday	24	22	11 a.m.	Wednesday
7	23	5 a.m.	Monday	25	22	5 p.m.	Thursday
6	23	10 a.m.	Tuesday	26	22	10 p.m.	Friday
5	22	4 p.m.	Wednesday	27	23	4 a.m.	Sunday
4	22	10 p.m.	Thursday	28	22	10 a.m.	Monday
3	23	4 a.m.	Saturday	29	22	4 p.m.	Tuesday
2	23	10 a.m.	Sunday	30	22	10 p.m.	Wednesday
1	22	3 p.m.	Monday	31	23	3 a.m.	Friday
CE				32	22	9 a.m.	Saturday
1	22	9 p.m.	Tuesday	33	22	3 p.m.	Sunday
2	23	3 a.m.	Thursday	34	22	9 p.m.	Monday
3	23	9 a.m.	Friday	35	23	3 a.m.	Wednesday
4	22	3 p m.	Saturday	36	22	9 a.m.	Thursday
5	22	8 p.m.	Sunday	37	22	2 p.m.	Friday
6	23	2 a.m.	Tuesday	38	22	8 p.m.	Saturday

* Midnight at the beginning of March 23.

This <u>First Table</u> tells us that in the year 34 A.D. the vernal equinox happened on Monday, March 22nd at 9pm according to Greenwich, England mean time (GMT) or 11pm Jerusalem time. The vernal equinox signals the end of the Hebrew year (*tekufah*). The full moon on this date, or on the next, confirms this time of the year.

SECOND TABLE
BCE

	FULL MOON			NEW MOON			
	On or next after date of equinox			On or preceding date of equinox		Date Following the equinox	
	Julian Greenwich Calendar			Julian Greenwich Calendar		Julian Greenwich Calendar	
Date	Date	Time	Day	Date	Time	Date	Time
25	April 3	4 a.m.	Thu.	March 19	Noon	April 18	4 a.m.
24	Mar. 23	9 p.m.	Mon.	March 8	2 p.m.	April 7	5 a.m.
23	April 11	9 p.m.	Sun.	Feb. 25	8 p.m.	Mar. 27	9 a.m.
22	April 1	6 a.m.	Fri.	Mar. 16	7 p.m.	April 15	6 a.m.
21	April 19	1 a.m.	Thu.	Mar. 5	11 a.m.	April 3	7 p.m.
20	April 8	3 a.m.	Mon.	Feb. 23	4 a.m.	Mar. 24	1 p.m.
19	Mar. 28	5 a.m.	Fri.	Mar. 14	4 a.m.	April 12	1 p.m.
18	April 16	0*	Thu.	Mar. 3	Noon	April 2	2 a.m.
17	April 4	Noon	Mon.	Mar. 21	8 a.m.	April 19	9 p.m.
16	Mar. 25	4 a.m.	Sat.	Mar. 10	8 a.m.	April 9	0*
15	April 13	5 a.m.	Fri.	Feb. 27	10 a.m.	Mar. 29	1 a.m.
14	April 2	7 p.m.	Tue.	Mar. 18	6 a.m.	April 16	7 p.m.
13	April 20	5 p.m.	Mon.	Mar. 6	6 p.m.	April 5	4 a.m.
12	April 9	9 p.m.	Fri.	Feb. 24	11 a.m.	Mar. 25	7 p.m.
11	Mar. 29	10 p.m.	Tue.	Mar. 15	Noon	April 13	8 p.m.
10	April 17	4 p.m.	Mon.	Mar. 5	2 a.m.	April 3	Noon
9	April 5	10 p.m.	Fri.	Mar. 22	11 p.m.	April 21	11 a.m.
8	Mar. 26	11 a.m.	Wed.	Mar. 12	3 a.m.	April 10	6 p.m.
7	April 14	Noon	Tue.	Mar. 1	3 a.m.	Mar. 30	7 p.m.
6	April 4	5 a.m.	Sun.	Mar. 19	9 p.m.	April 18	Noon
5	Mar. 23	6 p.m.	Thu.	Mar. 8	5 a.m.	April 6	5 p.m.
4	April 11	3 p.m.	Wed.	Feb. 25	6 p.m.	Mar. 27	4 a.m.
3	Mar. 31	6 p.m.	Sun.	Mar. 16	7 p.m.	April 15	4 a.m.
2	April 19	10 a.m.	Sat.	March 6	Noon	April 4	9 p.m.
1	April 7	Noon	Wed.	Feb. 24	0*	Mar. 24	Noon

CE

	FULL MOON			NEW MOON			
1	Mar. 27	9 p.m.	Sun.	Mar. 13	8 p.m.	April 12	9 a.m.
2	April 15	7 p.m.	Sat.	Mar. 2	10 p.m.	April 1	2 p.m.
3	April 5	Noon	Thu.	Mar. 21	3 p.m.	April 20	7 a.m.

4	Mar. 25	5 a.m	Tue.	Mar. 9	6 p.m.	April 8	9 a.m.
5	April 13	3 a.m.	Mon.	Feb. 27	3 a.m.	Mar. 28	2 p.m.
6	April 2	11 a.m.	Fri.	Mar. 18	3 a.m.	April 16	Noon
7	April 21	5 a.m.	Thu. (1)	Mar. 7	8 p.m.	April 6	4 a.m.
8	April 9	6 a.m.	Mon.	Feb. 25	Noon	Mar. 25	9 p.m.
9	Ma. 29	9 a.m.	Fri.	Mar. 15	10 a.m.	April 13	9 p.m.
10	April 17	6 a.m.	Thu.	Mar. 4	4 p.m.	April 3	6 a.m.
11	April 6	7 p.m.	Mon.	Mar. 23	10 a.m.	April 22	1 a.m.
12	Mar. 26	Noon	Sat.	Mar. 11	11 a.m.	April 10	3 a.m.
13	April 14	Noon	Fri.	Feb. 28	3 p.m.	Mar. 30	5 a.m.
14	April 4	2 a.m.	Wed.	Mar. 19	Noon	April 18	0*
15	Mar. 24	7 a.m.	Sun.	Mar. 9	2 a.m.	April 7	11 a.m.
16	April 11	0*	Sat.	Feb. 26	8 p.m.	Mar. 27	4 a.m.
17	Mar. 31	1 a.m.	Wed.	Mar. 16	8 p.m.	April 15	4 a.m.
18	April 18	7 p.m.	Mon.	Mar. 6	7 a.m.	April 4	7 p.m.
19	April 8	4 a.m.	Sat.	Feb. 23	Noon	Mar. 25	3 a.m.
20	Ma. 27	7 p.m.	Wed.	Mar. 13	5 a.m.	April 11	9 p.m.
21	April 15	8 p.m.	Tue.	Mar. 2	6 a.m.	Mar. 31	10 p.m.
22	April 5	Noon	Sun.	Mar. 21	1 a.m.	April 19	3 p.m.
23	Mar. 25	11 p.m.	Thu.	Mar. 10	11 a.m.	April 8	10 p.m.
24	April 12	6 p.m.	Wed.	Feb. 28	2 a.m.	Mar. 28	11 a.m.
25	April 1	7 p.m.	Sun.	Mar. 18	4 a.m.	April 16	Noon
26	April 20	Noon	Sat. (2)	Mar. 7	7 p.m.	April 6	5 a.m.
27	April 9	4 p.m.	Wed.	Feb. 25	4 a.m.	Mar. 26	5 p.m.
28	Mar. 29	3 a.m.	Mon.	Mar. 15	0*	April 13	2 p.m.
29	April 17	3 a.m.	Sun.	Mar. 4	0*	April 2	5 p.m.
30	April 6	8 p.m.	Thu.	Mar. 22	6 p.m.	April 21	9 a.m.
31	Mar. 27	11 a.m.	Tue.	Mar. 11	11 p.m.	April 10	Noon
32	April 14	9 a.m.	Mon.	Feb. 29	10 a.m.	Mar. 29	8 p.m.
33	April 3	3 p.m.	Fri.	Mar. 19	10 a.m.	April 17	7 p.m.
34	Mar. 23	3 p.m.	Tue.	Mar. 9	4 a.m.	April 7	Noon
35	April 11	8 a.m.	Mon.	Feb. 26	6 p.m.	March 28	4 a.m.
36	Mar. 30	2 p.m.	Fri.	Mar.16	3 p.m.	April 15	3 a.m.
37	April 18	Noon	Thu.	Mar. 5	7 p.m.	April 4	10 a.m.
38	April 8	3 a.m.	Tue.	Feb. 22	7 p.m.	Mar. 24	Noon

(1) Preceding Full Moon, March 22, 1 p.m.(2) Preceding Full Moon, March 21, 9 p.m.

* Midnight at the beginning of the given date.
(usno.navy.mil/USNO/astronomical-applications/astronomical-information-center)

The <u>Second Table</u> tells us in the year 34 A.D. that the full moon on March 23, at 3 p.m. confirms the vernal equinox, and that the first new moon following the vernal equinox was on April 7th at noon (GMT) and 2 p.m. (Jerusalem), which becomes the first day of the Hebrew New Year (Nisan 1). Fourteen days later, **April 22nd, or Nisan 14, would be Passover.**

This is not the End,

Jesus Has Fulfilled All,

And the New Has Begun!

"Behold, I am making all things new." And He said, "Write, for these words are faithful and true" (Revelation 21:5).

BIBLIOGRAPHY

(Aftermath.com) - Aftermath Services is the premier, nation-wide crime scene cleanup and biohazard remediation company. Aftermath's local offices are strategically located in and around major metro areas to service most cities across the US, with mobile team deployment immediately after we receive your call or online request for crime scene cleanup, trauma cleaning, unattended death cleanup, blood cleanup, or suicide cleanup. 877-695-4955 www.aftermath.com › content › human-decomposition

(Biblegateway.com) - Bible Gateway is a searchable online Bible in more than 200 versions and 70 languages that you can freely read, research, and reference anywhere. With a library of audio Bibles, a mobile app, devotionals, email newsletters, and other free resources, Bible Gateway equips you not only to *read* the Bible, but to *understand* it. The original multilingual searchable Bible website, Bible Gateway was started in 1993 by Nick Hengeveld, a student at Calvin College in Grand Rapids, MI, who had a visionary passion to make the Bible digitally accessible to everyone through the very new technology at the time called the Internet.
Passover: https://www.biblegateway.com/passage/?search=exodus+12%3A3-13&version=NASB
Abraham's Bosom: https://www.biblegateway.com/passage/?search=Luke+16%3A19-31&version=NASB

(Biblehub.com) - Bible hub is a production of the Online Parallel Bible Project. This project is privately owned and supported for the express purpose of sharing Bible study tools online. Most of our work is done by volunteers with an interest in using their technological skills to this end. Please see our contact page for additional information. The Online Parallel Bible Project began in 2004 as Bible.cc, which provided a parallel, verse by verse view of 8 translations. Soon, many new tools were developed to support the parallel site. These began as separate sites, but our feedback led us to develop a single integrated platform. Thus, in 2007 several sites were integrated to form Biblos.com and later BibleHub.com. https://biblehub.com/greek/3957.htm

(Biblestudytools.com) - BibleStudyTools.com is the largest free online Bible website for verse search and in-depth studies. Search verses using the translation and version you like with over 29 to choose from. Our rich online library includes well known and trusted commentaries including the popular Matthew Henry Commentary, concordances like Strong's Exhaustive Concordance and Naves Topical Concordance, Bible dictionaries, Biblical encyclopedias and historical Christian and church books including Fox's Book of Martyrs. Our library of resources also includes Bible reading plans, Parallel Bible, and many other additional Christian resources including dictionaries and encyclopedias. Copyright © 2020, Bible Study Tools. All rights reserved. Article Images Copyright © 2020 Getty Images unless otherwise indicated. https://www.biblestudytools.com/concordances/strongs-exhaustive-concordance

(Bibleworldhistory.com) - Bible World History - The History of the World from a Biblical Perspective ... The Bible World History chronology on this site is Copyright © 1999 by David Petrie. Please send all correspondence to the following email address: email@bibleworldhistory.com, David Petrie Sydney, Australia. http://www.bibleworldhistory.com/70Years.htm

(Brittannica.com) - Originally published: 1768, Publisher: Encyclopedia Britannica, Inc., Page count: 32,640 (15th edition, 2010), Editor: Hugh Chisholm
Countries: United Kingdom, United States

(Jewishencyclopedia.com) - This website contains the complete contents of the 12-volume Jewish Encyclopedia, which was originally published between 1901-1906. The Jewish Encyclopedia, which recently became part of the public domain, contains over 15,000 articles and illustrations. This online version contains the unedited contents of the original encyclopedia. Since the original work was completed almost 100 years ago, it does not cover a significant portion of modern Jewish History (e.g., the creation of Israel, the Holocaust, etc.). However, it does contain an incredible amount of information that is remarkably relevant today.

(cgsf.org) – Church of God Study Forum. This web site is dedicated to the study of that which is holy, that which is true- the Word of God, our source of wisdom, lamp to our feet and a light to our path. http://www.cgsf.org/dbeattie/calendar/?roman=34

(Chabad.org) - Judaism, Torah and Jewish Info - Chabad Lubavitch. https://www.chabad.org Official homepage for worldwide Chabad-Lubavitch movement that promotes Judaism and provides daily Torah lectures and Jewish insights. Chabad-Lubavitch is a philosophy, a movement, and an organization. Chabad is considered to be the most dynamic force in Jewish life today. https://www.chabad.org/library/article_cdo/aid/2263459/jewish/Hebrew-Months.htm

(Collinsdictionary.com) - Collins is a major publisher of Educational, Language and Geographic content, and have been publishing innovative, inspiring and informative books for over 200 years. Collins online dictionary and reference resources draw on the wealth of reliable and authoritative information about language, thanks to the extensive use of our corpora - vast databases of language - both in English and in other languages. These databases allow experienced Collins lexicographers to analyze how language is really used and monitor how language changes around the world. With the benefit of these corpora, our language specialists can be sure that they reflect accurate and authentic language throughout Collins dictionary and reference titles. https://www.collinsdictionary.com/us/dictionary/english/judaize

(Haaretz.com) - Haaretz is an independent daily newspaper with a broadly liberal outlook both on domestic issues and on international affairs. It has a journalistic staff of some 330 reporters, writers, and editors. The paper is perhaps best known for its Op-ed page, where its senior columnists - among them some of Israel's leading commentators and analysts - reflect on current events. Haaretz plays an important role in the shaping of public opinion and is read with care in government and decision-making circles. Haaretz was founded in Jerusalem in 1919 by a group of Zionist immigrants, mainly from Russia.
The established creation date: https://www.haaretz.com/jewish/3761-bce-the-world-is-created-1.5405777
The dating of the Hebrew calendar year: https://www.haaretz.com/jewish/.premium-the-secrets-of-the-hebrew-calendar-1.5304911

(Intercontinentalcog.org) - Intercontinental Church of God (ICG). The ICG has headquarters in Tyler, TX. The ICG is associated with the Garner Ted Armstrong Evangelistic Association (GTAEA). © 2021 The Intercontinental Church of God | P.O. Box 1117 • Tyler, Texas 75703 Passover Dates: intercontinentalcog.org/Appendix/Passover_dates_26-34_AD.php

(Jewishencyclopedia.com) - This website contains the complete contents of the 12-volume Jewish Encyclopedia, which was originally published between 1901-1906. The Jewish Encyclopedia, which recently became part of the public domain, contains over 15,000 articles and illustrations. This online version contains the unedited contents of the original encyclopedia. Since the original work was completed almost 100 years ago, it does not cover a significant portion of modern Jewish History (e.g., the creation of Israel, the Holocaust, etc.). However, it does contain an incredible amount of information that is remarkably relevant today. www.jewishencyclopedia.com › articles › 14292-tekufah

(Jewishgen.org) – JewishGen is a non-profit organization founded in 1987 as an international electronic resource for Jewish genealogy. In 2003, JewishGen became an affiliate of the Museum of Jewish Heritage – A Living Memorial to the Holocaust in New York City. It provides amateur and professional genealogists with the tools to research their Jewish family history and heritage. The Global Home for Jewish Genealogy, Edmond J. Safra Plaza, 36 Battery Place, New York, NY 10280. 646.494.5972, info@jewishgen.org © 2020, JewishGen, Inc. All rights reserved. Days of the Jewish Week: https://www.jewishgen.org/infofiles/m_calint.htm

(Jewishvirtuallibrary.org) - Encyclopedia of Jewish and Israeli history, politics and culture, with biographies, statistics, articles and documents on topics from anti-Semitism to Zionism. The American-Israeli Cooperative Enterprise (AICE) was established in 1993 as a nonprofit and nonpartisan organization to strengthen the U.S.-Israel relationship by emphasizing the fundamentals of the alliance — the values our nations share. © 1998 - 2020 American-Israeli Cooperative Enterprise.
First Fruits: https://www.jewishvirtuallibrary.org/first-fruits. Josephus: https://www.jewishvirtuallibrary.org/josephus-flavius.

(KJV) - The King James Version of the Bible. In 1604, at the request of King James I of England, representatives from the Church of England and leading English Puritans gathered together to discuss issues affecting the church in their day. Among those items for consideration was whether God would have them undertake the creation of a new Bible for the English-speaking world. King James approved plans for a new translation, and work began in 1607. Nearly 50 of the day's finest scholars, all from the Church of England, were organized into six groups for the task. Using the Bishop's Bible of 1568 as the basis for this revision, the Old Testament was translated from Hebrew and the New Testament from Greek. The completed work was then peer-reviewed before being sent to bishops and other church leaders for their examination, and ultimately to King James for his approval. In 1611, the King James Version Bible, also known as the Authorized Version, was published. https://www. thomasnelsonbibles.com/kjv/

(Ligonier.org) - Ligonier Ministries exists to proclaim, teach, and defend the holiness of God in all its fullness to as many people as possible. To that end, Ligonier's outreach today is manifold and worldwide. Having been founded by Dr. R.C. Sproul in 1971, Ligonier's teaching fellowship consists of theologians, pastors, and scholars who teach through Renewing Your Mind broadcasts, the Reformation Study Bible, Tabletalk magazine, books through the Reformation Trust Publishing division, and hundreds of teaching series. The ministry also offers an undergraduate degree program through Reformation Bible College. https://www.ligonier.org/learn/articles/new-covenant/

(Lexico.com) - Lexico.com is a new collaboration between Dictionary. com and Oxford University Press (OUP) to help users worldwide with everyday language challenges. Lexico is powered by Oxford's free English and Spanish dictionaries and features multi-language dictionary, thesaurus, and translation content. "Definition of Nisan". Oxford University Press. Lexico.com. 14 July 2020. https://www. lexico.com/definition/nisan.

(Lockman.org) – NASB Publisher: The Lockman Foundation. The Lockman Foundation is a nonprofit, nondenominational ministry dedicated to the translation, publication, and distribution of the New American Standard Bible (NASB). https://www.lockman.org/ nasb-bible-info/

(Merriam-Webster.com) - The Merriam-Webster.com Dictionary is a unique, regularly updated, online-only reference. Although originally based on Merriam-Webster's Collegiate® Dictionary, Eleventh Edition, the Merriam-Webster.com Dictionary has since been significantly updated and expanded with new entries and revised definitions. It also has additional content and engagement features specifically designed for the digital user.

(Myjewishlearning.com) - My Jewish Learning was launched in 2003 and is now a part of 70 Faces Media, the largest nonprofit, nondenominational Jewish media organization in North America. My Jewish Learning is all about empowering Jewish discovery for anyone interested in learning more. We offer thousands of articles, videos and other resources to help you navigate all aspects of Judaism and Jewish life — from food to history to beliefs and practices. This site is geared toward all backgrounds and level of knowledge. https://www.myjewishlearning.com/article/the-synagogue/

(ncbi.nlm.nih.gov) - Indian J Dermatol. 2009 Jul-Sep; 54(3): 290–292. doi: 10.4103/0019-5154.55645, PMCID: PMC2810702, PMID: 20161867 Published since 1955, Indian Journal of Dermatology (IJD®), (ISSN: Print- 0019-5154, Online - 1998-3611) is the oldest living journal of Dermatology in Asia which is being published uninterruptedly under the same name since its inception and continues to be one of the pioneer medical journals from India. It is, in fact, one of the oldest peer-reviewed journals dedicated to this particular discipline. https://www.ncbi.nlm.nih.gov/pmc/articles/PMC2810702/

(Oxfordbiblicalstudies.com) - Oxford Biblical Studies Online brings together a range of authoritative Bible texts, up-to-date scholarly commentary, and reference materials for a wide range of research and study activities. The content is structured with a breadth and depth that will benefit students, specialists, faculty and divines, scholars in a variety of disciplines, and reference librarians. http://www.oxfordbiblicalstudies.com/article/opr/t94/e1172

(Ptv.org) - Established in 1996, Pathway to Victory serves as the broadcast ministry of Dr. Robert Jeffress and the First Baptist Church of Dallas, Texas. Pathway to Victory stands for truth and exists to pierce the darkness with the light of God's Word through the most effective media available, including television, radio, print, and digital media. Through Pathway to Victory, Dr. Robert Jeffress spreads the Good News of Jesus Christ to a lost and hurting people, confronts an ungodly culture with God's truth, and equips the saints to apply scripture to their everyday lives. https://ptv.org/devotional/limitations-of-the-old-covenant/

(usno.navy.mil) - United States Naval Observatory Astronomical Applications Department. USNO strengthens national security and critical infrastructure by serving as DoD's authoritative source for the positions and motion of celestial bodies, motions of the Earth, and precise time. USNO provides tailored products, performs relevant research, develops leading edge technologies and instrumentation, and operates state of the art systems in support of the U.S. Navy, DoD, Federal Agencies, international partners, and the general public. USNO Info: https://www.usno.navy.mil/USNO/astronomical-applications/astronomical-information-center

(YLT) - The Young's Literal Translation Bible text designated YLT is from the 1898 Young's Literal Translation by Robert Young who also compiled Young's Analytical Concordance. This is an extremely literal translation that attempts to preserve the tense and word usage as found in the original Greek and Hebrew writings. The text was scanned from a reprint of the 1898 edition as published by Baker Book House, Grand Rapids Michigan. The book is still in print and may be ordered from Baker Book House. Obvious errors in spelling or inconsistent spellings of the same word were corrected in the computer edition of the text. https://www.biblegateway.com/versions/Youngs-Literal-Translation-YLT-Bible/

THE
FULFILLMENT
OF
PASSOVER
AND
THE
TIMELINE OF THE CRUCIFIXION
OF
JESUS
CHRIST

Printed in the United States
by Baker & Taylor Publisher Services